OVERCOMING MENTAL BATTLES IN MINISTRY

FIND HELP IN TIMES OF NEED AS YOU SET YOUR MIND ON THINGS ABOVE

MOISÉS ESTEVES

Formatted and edited by Katie Erickson, KatieEricksonEditing.com

ISBN: 979-8-9909462-0-0

Dedication

This book is dedicated to my wife, Maryjane,
my greatest encourager in ministry.

The book is also dedicated to our children
Marcos, Daniel, Rebeca, and Priscilla.
May you always know how much you are loved.

Foreword

As a full-time leader in a Christian organization, I've often found myself asking Moisés, "When will your book be available?" I have heard Moisés teach on this subject on several occasions, and I knew that more people needed to have access to this excellent resource. There is such a great need for practical and biblical advice to the Christian community generally and to those in ministry specifically on this important subject. I truly believe that Moisés is uniquely prepared and equipped to write such a book. I personally have witnessed the effects of discouragement, the battles lost that could have been won, and, tragically, the departures from ministry due to unaddressed mental and spiritual conflicts.

It is my great pleasure to write the foreword to a publication that addresses a deeply felt need. *Overcoming Mental Battles in Ministry* stands out as a vital source of wisdom and guidance for those navigating the complexities of ministry life. Having known Moisés for many years, I can attest to his profound understanding and compassion for the mental and spiritual challenges ministry workers face. Our paths have crossed in various capacities—I've served alongside him in different groups, traveled with him to numerous countries, and witnessed firsthand his unwavering commitment to encourage friends, coworkers, and family members in their journey. Moisés' openness about his own struggles and his commitment to

God's Word to illuminate the way through mental battles are both inspiring and grounding. His rich experiences, both as a leader and a humble servant, are deeply woven into the fabric of this insightful book. Moisés has a heart for those in ministry and a genuine desire to support their journey in staying spiritually, emotionally, and mentally healthy. His book is more than a manual; it's a testimony to his life's work in standing alongside others in overcoming the challenges that often accompany God's call.

Reflecting on over 25 years of service in full-time ministry, I've become increasingly aware of the importance of overcoming the mental battles that accompany our God-given calling. These challenges are not merely hurdles; they are opportunities to grow deeper in our faith and, ultimately, to triumph in Christ. It's a path that demands not only insight and patience, but also practical, biblical guidance along the way. *Overcoming Mental Battles in Ministry* emerges as that guiding light, resonating with those of us on the front lines of spiritual service, but also for every believer who seeks to live a life of integrity. In my own journey alongside Moisés as I witnessed his dedication to uplift and guide, I've seen how essential it is to address these battles head-on, armed with faith and an open heart. This book provides the wisdom and support that I and many others have sought in moments of doubt and struggle.

This book distinguishes itself through a thorough exploration of essential topics for maintaining mental and spiritual health in ministry. Addressing issues from the dangers of incorrect thinking and the weight of expectations to navigating authority and avoiding deception, Moisés provides more than insights—he offers practical counsel. Each chapter gives opportunity for both reflection and growth: mirroring our innermost struggles and mapping a path to victory through faith and wisdom. Moisés' method of blending personal stories with biblical truths offers not just solutions, but a comforting hand to those feeling overwhelmed. Through his narrative, he reminds us that we are not alone in our struggles, providing a source of solace and strength drawn from the very core of our faith. His approach is akin to having a trusted mentor by your side, guiding you through the storms with grace and wisdom. What makes *Overcoming Mental Battles in Ministry* invaluable is its deep understanding that the journey of ministry is both intensely personal and universally challenging. Moisés' voice serves as a beacon, directing us toward the light of understanding and resilience, ensuring that we, as Christian workers, can continue to serve with passion and purpose, unhindered by the mental battles that once may have held us back.

We have before us a road map for overcoming the mental and spiritual battles that can deter us from our calling. It's a testimony to the strength found in vulnerability, the power of God's Word, and the unbreakable spirit of those called to serve. As someone who has navigated these battles alongside Moisés, I can attest to the transformative power of the insights contained within this book. It is a must-read for anyone in ministry, providing the tools and encouragement needed to face our battles with courage and emerge victorious.

In closing, I wholeheartedly recommend *Overcoming Mental Battles in Ministry* to all engaged in ministry work, from seasoned pastors to volunteers or those simply looking to support spiritual leaders. Crafted with profound insights and heartfelt encouragement by Moisés Esteves, this book marks a significant milestone. As we celebrate its release, let's also embrace the challenge of overcoming our mental battles, equipped with the knowledge and direction found in these pages. May this book serve as a catalyst for overcoming mental battles in ministry for you as it did for me.

Iulian Mangalagiu
European Regional Director
Child Evangelism Fellowship

Acknowledgments

I want to thank several friends and leaders who read the manuscript of this book and offered valuable suggestions for improvement: Skip Hessel, David Tosi, Lynne Herlein, Gerd-Walter Buskies, and Iulian Mangalagiu, who also graciously wrote the foreword. Casey Pontius was very helpful in pursuing permissions for quotes. A special thank you to Cora Tucker who was a big help in editing earlier versions of the manuscript, researching illustrations, bibliography, document management, and much more. Thank you also to Katie Erickson who did a great job as editor and with the layout and cover of the book.

I would like to acknowledge the extraordinary debt I owe to the hundreds of leaders I worked with over the last thirty years. I learned so much from each one. We sharpened each other in Christian service. Thank you!

Table of Contents

Introduction

In 1993 God led us to leave Portugal, the country where I was born, and come to the USA to lead the ministry of a children's organization in a New England state. Those early years of ministry were positive with good relationships with many volunteers, pastors, teens, board members, staff, children, etc.

In 1997 I received an invitation to leave that state and go serve at the international headquarters in the center of the country. The board members in that state were not happy with this change, and they became upset with me. Things got more and more tense, to the point that it required the national director to come to that state on an Easter Sunday afternoon to have a mediation meeting. The board members were there, the three pastors in the advisory board were there, plus the national director and me. The board members expressed their unhappiness with my departure. They felt betrayed. These were my friends. We worked together for several years. Most of the meeting I kept my head down. I didn't defend myself. I cried about half the time.

Why is it that when you are trying with all your heart to serve God, you find yourself in these situations? My mind was racing. Besides this external battle, there was a battle in my mind. What was I going to do? Should I leave the ministry? Should I stay? I don't remember secular work being this painful. How my mind engaged that trial was going to make the difference between serving God in ministry for many years or leaving ministry.

Fast-forward a good number of years. I have fought many mental battles while serving the Lord in that same ministry for three decades. This international Christian organization has more than 3,500 full-time staff. In the different roles I have served, I have also witnessed many ministry staff and leaders fight many mental battles. Or, to be more accurate, I guess what I saw were the results of those mental battles.

Some people come into ministry as a volunteer, as full-time or part-time staff, or even with a lifetime calling for full-time ministry service only to leave a few years later broken and defeated. Many leave secular work to come into ministry with great expectations. "Certainly, serving God with all these wonderful Christians is going to be an amazing experience." Soon, though, they discover that many times ministry contains problems and battles. Sometimes you feel like you go from battle to battle. After many years serving in ministry, I remember talking to my supervisor several times about what I experienced and called "battle fatigue." This is a sense that you are exhausted, spent, and have nothing left to give to others. The battles have sucked the life out of you.

Helping people involved in ministry experience victory through the mental battles they face is the purpose of this book. While we live in this broken world, the mental battles are not going to disappear. We are certainly going to face them, but we don't have to be defeated by them. It is true that all Christians experience spiritual mental battles and that these principles can also be helpful to them. It is true that all Christians should be involved in some kind of ministry service to the Lord, and in that sense, they can all benefit from these principles. However, the burden I carry as I write is to provide help especially for those involved in full-time or volunteer ministry.

In this book I address many different topics. Each topic falls into one of three categories: battles within yourself, battles with other people, and battles with the enemy of our souls. Some of the battles within that we will cover are tied to how we manage expectations and fears, how we see the future, our understanding of patience and waiting, how we resolve disappointments, and how we deal with wrong thinking. Concerning battles with people, we will discuss quarrels and fights and the power of love, forgiveness, and unity. We will also look at the original mental battle and how to resist the enemy of our souls. I want to alert ministry leaders to the different types of mental battles they can face in ministry and offer some help so that they may experience a measure of victory in those battles.

I am a firm believer in academic Bible training as preparation for ministry. I would love to see Bible colleges or universities provide more help with how to have victory in ministry mental battles. This is different from methods for conflict resolution. It is true that conflict can wear people down like few other things do and that conflict fuels mental battles in people. What I am talking about is not the issues outside of the ministry leader that he or she encounters. What I am talking about is how those events impact the person's mind and how the person's mind interacts with the world around them.

God has placed a burden on my soul to help ministry leaders to "…take every thought captive to obey Christ" (2 Cor. 10:5) and stay in effective ministry for a lifetime. Much of this content comes from God's Word and from lessons learned by observing my own heart and interacting with hundreds of ministry staff over the years. My prayer is that this book will be of help to you as you face your own mental battles in ministry.

Defining Mental Battles in Ministry

In March 2022 Barna Group came out with new research about pastor burnout in the USA. It concluded that as of that month 42% of pastors considered quitting full-time ministry in the previous year, giving as top reasons: too much stress, loneliness in ministry, political divisions, and a negative effect of the pastor's role on the family. Barna Group states, "Over half the pastors who have considered quitting full-time ministry (56%) say 'the immense stress of the job' has factored into their thoughts on leaving. Beyond these general stressors, two in five pastors (43%) say, 'I feel lonely and isolated.'"[1] The study goes on to report on many other reasons, but these are the top reasons over which pastors consider quitting.

I believe people in ministry experience many mental battles. Every believer fights mental battles, but people in ministry experience those more intensely. Many win those battles and continue, focused on ministry. Others leave the ministry defeated. Many are the stories; every story is unique, but most of them contain mental battles. I would like to define ministry mental battles.

I think much of our suffering from ministry-related issues comes from the subtle, yet real change in our thoughts when we are not setting our mind on the things of God, but on the things of man. Paul wrote to the Colossians: "If then you have been raised with Christ, seek the things that are above, where Christ is, seated at the right hand of God. Set your minds on things that are above, not on things that are on earth" (Col. 3:1, 2). What precipitates the mental battle many times might be a grumpy person, a reluctant coworker, an illness, or an unexpected problem. All these are external circumstances, and it is easy for us to conclude that that person is at fault for the way I feel. In truth, the most important thing is not the external circumstances, but how we react to the external circumstances. The key is what happens in my mind as I process the external circumstances. Am I going to set my mind on the things of God as I think about that issue, or am I going to set my mind on the things of man as I think about that issue? Is my perspective going to be vertical or horizontal? Is my viewpoint going to be divine or earthly? One leads to peace and joy, and the other leads to sadness and bad decisions.

One good way to illustrate this is by looking at a particular time in the Apostle Peter's life. One day Jesus was having a conversation with His disciples. "He said to them, "But who do you say that I am?" (Matt. 16:15). Peter steps forward and responds, "You are the Christ, the Son of the living God." Jesus was delighted with Peter's answer and told him, "Blessed are you, Simon Bar-Jonah! For flesh and blood has not revealed this to you, but my Father who is in heaven." That statement revealed that this idea that came upon Peter's mind and out of his mouth had its origin in God.

A few moments later, "Jesus began to show his disciples that he must go to Jerusalem and suffer many things from the elders and chief priests and scribes, and be killed, and on the third day be raised" (Matt. 16:21). Peter was not happy to hear that Jesus was going to die. Because Peter thought that this was a bad idea, he began reacting based on those thoughts. He even rebuked the Savior: "And Peter took him aside and began to rebuke him, saying, 'Far be it from you, Lord! This shall never happen to you.'"

I have seen ministry leaders so convinced that something is wrong that they will act very strongly against it. They will even violate some biblical principles (such as rebuking the Savior in Peter's example) to make their case. They can be wrong about it even though they are convinced they are right. The pattern is many times the same. Wrong thinking leads to strong negative emotions, and those lead to wrong actions. The Lord Jesus knew what was taking place, and He told Peter, "Get behind me, Satan! You are a hindrance to me. For you are not setting your mind on the things of God, but on the things of man." Jesus revealed that this thought came from Satan. It came out of the Apostle Peter's mouth, but its origin was the devil. From Peter's perspective, this thought was good. It was a bad idea for Jesus to die, so Peter told Jesus that.

Jesus' response contained two sentences. The first sentence was a rebuke to Satan, the one who threw that flaming dart (Eph. 6:16) at Peter: "Get behind me, Satan! You are a hindrance to me." Keep in mind that he was in the middle of a dialogue with Peter and most likely was looking at Peter as they were talking. Jesus was rebuking the originator of this idea. What about the second sentence? Was it directed at Satan, at Peter, or at both? "For you are not setting your mind on the things of God, but on the things of man." I think that sentence was directed at Peter. We know that Satan never sets his mind on the things of God. It is Peter that has the choice to set his mind on the things of God or on the things of man. By repeating Satan's thought, Peter was not setting his mind on the things of God (the atoning death of Christ), but on the things of man (preventing Jesus' death and the disciples' apparent loss). This is the great Apostle Peter who preached the Gospel boldly, resulting in thousands saved. This is the apostle who pioneered ministry to the Gentiles. If the great Apostle Peter could commit such an error, any of us could, too.

This is a clear case of a mental battle in ministry. Another example also involving Peter is when he asked the Lord to walk on water (Matt. 14:22-33). As Peter came toward Jesus, he was able to walk on water. As long as his focus was on the Savior, he rose above the circumstances. Once his focus shifted toward the wind, toward the circumstances and away from Christ, he began to sink. The circumstances around him overcame him. Of course, the Lord reached out to him and rescued him, but moments later the Lord told him, "You of little faith… why did you doubt?" What a perfect illustration of Colossians 3:2, "Set your minds on things that are above, not on things that are on earth." In one moment, Peter has his mind set on things that are above, the Lord Jesus, and the next moment he has his mind set on things that are on earth, the wind. Notice how his emotions and decisions are closely connected to where he sets his mind. It is the same with you and me.

Throughout this book we are going to seek to understand this dynamic topic and provide biblical helps to achieve victory in our ministry mental battles. Satan desires to make us miserable in ministry and convince us to stop ministering. God desires for us to have peace and joy in ministry, even in the midst of trials, and to be steadfast in it. That pretty much describes mental battles. Your mind is the battlefield, and no one is immune.

The Blindness of Wrong Thinking

After living in Portugal for many years, my family and I moved to the USA, where at the age of 31 I started working with a ministry in Vermont. By then, I had bought and sold two condos in Portugal: one in the Lisbon area and another in the Porto area. When I sold those condos, I made a small profit. After arriving in Vermont, I was ready to buy a house for my family inOrwell, a small town of 900 people. The larger nearby city with more places to shop was Middlebury, about 30 minutes away. A friend of mine from Vermont heard about my idea to buy a house out in the countryside, and he said not to do it. He told me that later when it was time to sell, I would lose money. My experience (even though it was in Portugal) told me the right thing was to buy and expect the property to build some value until I would sell it in the future. My mind was set. I disregarded the counsel of my friend. Years later, when we were going to move to Missouri, we were trying to sell the house. It wouldn't sell. We lowered the price several times, and it took us a full year to sell the house. Eventually, a storm came through the area and damaged another house where a large family lived. They were suddenly looking for a house, and they ended up buying our house. God used a storm to help us sell the house. When it was all said and done, we lost quite a bit of money on the house transaction. My friend had been right all along. Human beings are quite peculiar. We can feel very strongly that something is right when that thing is wrong. Someone will offer advice, but we ignore it because in our minds we are right. That is a form of wrong thinking.

Everyone struggles with wrong thinking. it can happen in business or in any area of life. When it happens in ministry, it is a very difficult thing for the leader and for those who follow that leader. I have had my share of wrong thinking over the years. Wrong thinking is one the most common mental battles ministry leaders experience. A biblical example is a church leader named Diotrephes. Diotrephes had a problem with wrong thinking, and we read about him in 3 John. "I have written something to the church, but Diotrephes, who likes to put himself first, does not acknowledge our authority. So, if I come, I will bring up what he is doing, talking wicked nonsense against us. And not content with that, he refuses to welcome the brothers, and also stops those who want to and puts them out of the church" (3 John 9-10).

John wrote that Diotrephes liked to put himself first, he did not acknowledge the authority of the Apostle John, he spoke "wicked nonsense" against John and his team members, he did not welcome other believers, and he kicked people out of the church. We look at these actions and know they are not right. Behind these actions is a mind full of wrong thinking.

How can good Christian leaders end up with wrong thinking? The devil is an expert at causing good people to think incorrectly. He is the great deceiver. No human being is immune. No one! Add to that the fact that human hearts are easily deceived, and you have a dangerous combination. "The heart is deceitful above all things, and desperately sick; who can understand it?" (Jer. 17:9).

Can Satan deceive believers into wrong thinking? Absolutely! This is what Paul wrote to the believers in Corinth: "But I am afraid that as the serpent deceived Eve by his cunning, your thoughts will be led astray from a sincere and pure devotion to Christ" (2 Cor. 11:3). As we examined in an earlier chapter, Satan led the Apostle Peter into wrong thinking in Matthew 16 when he told Jesus he did not have to go to Jerusalem and die on the cross. If an apostle can be led into wrong thinking, any Christian can. Matthew 16:23 presents a definition of wrong thinking: "You are not setting your mind on the things of God, but on the things of man." This warped thinking happens when believers stop focusing their thoughts on the things of God (His Word) and begin thinking on the things of man (the flesh and the world). This can be very subtle.

The consequences of wrong thinking are devastating; it leads to negative emotions and to wrong decisions. Peace goes out the window and is replaced with turmoil. "For the mind set on the flesh is death, but the mind set on the Spirit is life and peace…" (Rom. 8:6). God calls peace in our hearts a referee in Colossians 3:15: "And let the peace of Christ rule in your hearts…." The Greek word translated to "rule" means to act as umpire or a referee. Peace in the heart of the believer is like a check engine light in a vehicle. When the heart of the believer has no peace and is filled with turmoil, that is a sign that wrong thinking has entered the mind.

There is only one antidote for wrong thinking: the truth of God's Word. "For the word of God is… able to judge the thoughts and intentions of the heart" (Heb. 4:12). The more time we spend in

God's Word, the more our thinking is cleansed. Jesus prayed for His followers and said, "Sanctify them in the truth; your word is truth" (John 17:17). Jesus stated, "and you will know the truth, and the truth will set you free" (John 8:32). Jesus was saying that only the truth of God's Word can set us free from the lies and deception that the enemy plants in our minds.

Let's go back to Diotrephes. Since wrong thoughts are closely related to a person's wrong words and wrong actions, we can easily imagine his wrong thoughts. Most likely, Diotrephes entertained thoughts that the church belonged to him, he was the highest authority, and he was the protector of the church. Diotrephes likely had the classic savior-complex syndrome. So many times, wrong thinking leads to this syndrome: "If things are not done my way (the right way), the ministry will be lost."

Let's bring some biblical truth into his thinking.

- Diotrephes thought the church belonged to him. The church belongs to Christ. "And he is the head of the body, the church. He is the beginning, the firstborn from the dead, that in everything he might be preeminent" (Col. 1:18). The church is Christ's, and we are humble servants of Jesus.
- Diotrephes thought that he was the highest authority in the church. "And Jesus came and said to them, 'All authority in heaven and on earth has been given to me'" (Matt. 28:18). Jesus is the highest authority. The rest of us are His meek servants and servants of one another. We are not ministry owners. Christ is the owner, and we are unworthy stewards.
- Diotrephes thought that he was the protector of the church and that he ought to decide who stayed and who was kicked out. Jesus is the real protector of the church: "…I will build

my church, and the gates of hell shall not prevail against it" (Matt. 16:18b).

- Diotrephes had a savior mentality. He probably thought, "If I don't do all these things for the church, the church is going to fail. I have to save the church." The position of savior is taken. The church already has a Savior: "…Christ is the head of the church, his body, and is himself its Savior" (Eph. 5:23b). The savior mentality is nothing but pride disguised in religiosity.

Sometimes good Christians and good Christian leaders who know the Word of God are so deceived that they can't snap out of it. They read the Word, but interpret it through their deception and continue to be stuck in wrong thinking. After all, the problem with deception is that you don't realize you are deceived. God made provision for those Christian leaders to have help. If you are in a leadership position that impacts many people and you are deceived, the ministry can suffer.

God's additional safeguard from leaders' wrong thinking is a multitude of counselors. "Where there is no guidance, a people falls, but in an abundance of counselors there is safety" (Prov. 11:14). The word "safety" in the Hebrew means "deliverance" or "salvation." This helps us understand the importance of many godly counselors. "Without counsel plans fail, but with many advisers they succeed" (Prov. 15:22). Listening to many counselors will provide the ministry with success and safety; it will provide safety from wrong decisions made by wrong-thinking leaders.

Things still get more complicated. The temptation is for wrong-thinking leaders to approach counselors that think like them and avoid counselors that will push back on their ideas. This happens so many times. Healthy leaders welcome pushback. They welcome the opportunity to have their ideas verified by the wisdom of many leaders, of key stakeholders in the decision being made. No one has all the knowledge. No individual has all the spiritual gifts. The Holy Spirit spread the spiritual gifts needed for the functioning of the body to many people to force us to have to depend on others and not to think that we can do it all. Christ is the Head, and the body has many members that need each other. Leaders need people around them that push back constructively on their ideas. Notice that God's solution is an "abundance" of counselors and "many" advisers.

It is important to ask counsel from the right people. In 1 Kings 12 the new king, Rehoboam, takes counsel from the older wise leaders, men who had stood in the presence of his father, Solomon. They had heard for many years the God-given wisdom of Solomon. Rehoboam also took counsel from his young friends. Then it was decision time. "But he abandoned the counsel that the old men gave him and took counsel with the young men who had grown up with him and stood before him" (1 Kings 12:8). He followed the counsel of his buddies. He made a bad decision, and as a result, the kingdom was divided. He should have followed the counsel of the older, wiser, more experienced leaders in the kingdom. If he had followed their counsel, the kingdom could have remained unified. So many times, decisions made under the counsel of the wrong voices lead to very negative results.

My experience is that when godly leaders don't agree with my ministry idea or direction, often it means the Holy Spirit is trying to tell me something, to guide me, to warn me, or to direct me. The leader with an idea he is trying to implement should not see pushback as an obstacle to go around, but as the Lord giving additional insight and guidance in the matter.

God gave us a wonderful safeguard to save leaders from wrong thinking and wrong decisions: the truth of God's Word. In addition to His Word, God provides wisdom, safety, and success in the multitude of advisers. Great damage can be made to a Christian organization when these spiritual principles are ignored. Are you following this principle in your leadership? The next time you find yourself with a troubled heart and a racing mind, it could be that you are struggling with wrong thinking and you don't know it. Study God's Word and run to a multitude of godly counselors. Christian leaders must "take every thought captive to the obedience of Christ" (2 Cor. 10:5). Is your mind dwelling on wrong thinking? Based on the principles discussed in this chapter, is your mind dwelling on things that lead to wrong thinking? If you aren't sure, ask God to reveal His truth through your personal study. Are there godly individuals that you talk with to ensure that you are thinking biblically?

The Tough Business of People-Pleasing

The advent of social media has brought the trap of people-pleasing to new heights. So many people crave affirmation from others that they post just the right message so others will be pleased and "like" what they shared. At times when you share a personal conviction about something, some people may criticize you, and then you feel bad because instead of receiving the affirmation you longed for, you got the opposite: condemnation. People quickly learn to not push back on the group opinion because they don't want to experience rejection. Their desire to please people actually leads them to change their positions on a variety of topics. There are powerful forces at play with people-pleasing.

People-pleasing is a tough business. Many people in ministry are caught in the trap of pleasing people. This can be the source of a powerful mental battle. What is the problem in wanting to please people? Well, it's an impossible mission. People's opinions, positions, and feelings change like the wind. Here are a few examples. The people of Lystra declared that Paul and Barnabas were gods in the likeness of men and wanted to offer sacrifices to them. Later that day the same crowd stoned Paul and Barnabas, nearly killing them (Acts 14:11-19). In another instance, the people of Malta thought Paul was a murderer. Then within a few hours, they changed their minds and claimed that he was a god (Acts 28:4-6). Many in the crowd that cried out "Hosanna" to the Lord Jesus as he entered Jerusalem were also the same ones who cried out "Crucify him" just a brief time later (John 12:13; Matt. 27:20-23).

Let's consider a tragic biblical example of people-pleasing that influenced a leader. God had told King Saul to destroy the Amalekites, their people, and their animals. This was an act of judgment from a merciful and holy God. God had patiently waited hundreds of years for the evil of the Amalekites to get to the point that it demanded judgment. The waiting was in hope that they would repent. However, instead of destroying everything, Saul spared the Amalekite king and saved many of the animals. Basically, he disobeyed God. When the prophet Samuel confronted King Saul about his disobedience, Saul responded, "…the people spared the best of the sheep and of the oxen to sacrifice to the Lord your God, and the rest we have devoted to destruction" (1 Sam. 15:15). Saul justified his disobedience by saying these animals were to be sacrificed to the Lord. Someone could say that this reason had some merit. Wasn't it a wonderful thing to desire to sacrifice animals to the Lord? Nevertheless, was this the real reason Saul disobeyed God? No. So often, the reason given is a façade, hiding the real reason. Later, after the prophet Samuel described the consequences of Saul's sin, the real reason emerged. "Saul said to Samuel, 'I have sinned, for I have transgressed the commandment of the Lord and your words, because I feared the people and obeyed their voice'" (1 Sam. 15:24).

People-pleasing or the fear of displeasing people was the real reason King Saul disobeyed God and lost his kingdom. At its core, people-pleasing is fueled by the fear of men. Maybe the soldiers put pressure on the king because those animals were perfect and were worth a lot of money. Why destroy them? That didn't make sense. The Bible doesn't tell us what the dialogue was like between the soldiers and the king, but we can easily imagine it. The soldiers put pressure on the king, and Saul began fighting a mental battle trying to decide if he was going to please God or please his men. We know which way he decided. The king of Israel feared the people. He felt that he had to please them, to listen to their voice and do what they wanted. Because of that he lost his kingdom. People-pleasing can become a trap.

You might be wondering, "But is it not important for people around you to have a good opinion of you and be pleased with you as a ministry leader?" Absolutely! As Paul listed the requirements to be an elder in the church, he included this: "Moreover, he must be well thought of by outsiders…" (1 Tim. 3:7). The only difference is that we don't pursue that. We pursue the approval and pleasure of God, and one of the outcomes is that most people around us will be pleased with us as well. But some will not. As always, the Lord Jesus is our perfect example: "And Jesus increased in wisdom and in stature and in favor with God and man" (Luke 2:52). We must do all we can to have a good reputation, but we must do that in a way that primarily pleases God.

Beware that if you are focused on pleasing God, you might end up with one or two people that oppose you, not because you are doing bad things, but because you are living a godly life. "Indeed, all who desire to live a godly life in Christ Jesus will be persecuted" (2 Tim. 3:12). What shall we do about those who are our enemies? Should we change what we do? No! We continue to focus on pleasing God and let God deal with them. "When a man's ways please the Lord, he makes even his enemies to be at peace with him" (Prov. 16:7).

Even if God does not deal with them immediately, or even if it appears He is not dealing with them, we must continue to focus on God's agenda.

A great example of this outside pressure was Nehemiah. He was on a God-given mission to rebuild the walls of Jerusalem. Many of the people loved Nehemiah and helped him on this most noble task. He also experienced opposition from Sanballat, Tobiah, and Geshem, who tried many times to stop the construction of the walls. Later, even some of his countrymen were unhappy with Nehemiah due to some of his reforms. Nehemiah's ultimate success resulted from him being consumed with pleasing God and not with pleasing people.

David is another example of a leader who was not influenced by people-pleasing. King Saul spent years seeking to find David so he could kill him. It was very difficult for David and his men, as they had to be constantly on the run. Those years were extremely difficult and very stressful. One day, King Saul was out looking for David with three thousand men. Saul needed a personal break and entered a cave to relieve himself. He was there alone. At least, he thought he was alone. Deeper into the cave were David and his men. They knew Saul was in the cave by himself. "And the men of David said to him, 'Here is the day of which the Lord said to you, "Behold, I will give your enemy into your hand, and you shall do to him as it shall seem good to you"'" (1 Sam. 24:4). David's men put pressure on David to kill Saul and to end their stressful lifestyle as runaways. It made sense to them. To them it was obvious that God had brought Saul into the cave for that purpose. Would David listen to his men? Would he kill Saul? Would he please his men?

David decided not to please his men. "He said to his men, 'The Lord forbid that I should do this thing to my lord, the Lord's anointed, to put out my hand against him, seeing he is the Lord's anointed.' So David persuaded his men with these words and did not permit them to attack Saul…" (1 Sam. 24:6-7). David chose to please God. He knew that Saul had been anointed by the Lord to serve as king and that only God could remove Saul. Instead of killing Saul, "David arose and stealthily cut off a corner of Saul's robe" (1 Sam. 24:4). Later he spoke to Saul about it and confessed it was wrong to have done that against the king. He was sensitive to God when others may have thought his actions were justified. David was determined to please God rather than men. We see this happen several times in his life. This is one of the reasons the Lord spoke of David as "a man after his own heart" (1 Sam. 13:14).

Our focus in life and ministry should be foremost to please God and obey Him. One might ask, "How am I sure that my life is pleasing to God?" The Apostle Paul penned the answer: "Finally, then, brothers, we ask and urge you in the Lord Jesus, that as you received from us how you ought to walk and to please God, just as you are doing, that you do so more and more. For you know what instructions we gave you through the Lord Jesus" (1 Thess. 4:1-3). When some people are not happy with you because of your decision to please God, encourage them and explain the rationale of your decision. When you face some discomfort because of your decision, wait on the Lord and stay the course. It is not wrong to seek to please your supervisor or leader as long as you are obeying God at the same time. Remember the midwives in Egypt? When Pharaoh ordered them to throw the Israeli baby boys into the river, they quietly decided, "No, we will not do that." They lied to Pharaoh to protect those baby boys, and because of their actions, God blessed them with their own families.

Obedience to God's Word, regardless of the consequences, is the sure way to please God. The approval of men pales in comparison to hearing from our God at the end of our lives, "Well done, good and faithful servant." We need to overcome the people-pleasing mental battles. Someone has said, "We live for an audience of One." If God is pleased, we need to be pleased as well. Are you seeking the approval of God or of men?

The Roller Coaster of Expectations

My wife grew up in Vermont, where people have dryers for their clothes. Winters are very cold in Vermont. When we got married, we moved to Portugal, the country where I was born. That beautiful Southern European country has an average of 300 sunny days each year. Most people there don't need and don't have dryers. Everyone hangs their clothes outside, and they dry pretty quickly. When we had one child in cloth diapers, I knew my wife would love to have a dryer, but she was managing without having one. One Christmas I searched for a dryer, found one, bought it, and gave it to her for Christmas. Her reaction of joy and excitement was amazing. She was so happy she shed tears of joy. She was not expecting a dryer, and that made the gift so much more precious.

On the other hand, if she had been expecting a dryer and I was not able to find it, she would have been very disappointed. It is easy for human beings to have expectations. We have mental expectations of relationships, our children, our spouses, our coworkers, our bosses, sports teams, vacations, Christmas, and just about everything under the sun. We create these expectations without even thinking about it. There is only one problem: Most of the time we have no control in meeting those expectations. When expectations go unmet, we are disappointed and sad. Expectations are a factory of mental battles.

The prophet Jonah had received a call from God to go to Nineveh: "Arise, go to Nineveh, that great city, and call out against it, for their evil has come up before me" (Jonah 1:2). Jonah thought about it, and his expectations kicked in. He knew that the Ninevites were evil people, and he expected God to judge them. He also knew that God is "…a gracious God and merciful, slow to anger and abounding in steadfast love, and relenting from disaster" (Jonah 4:2). In his mind he feared God would give mercy to the Ninevites, but Jonah expected judgment. Not wanting to take the risk, Jonah ran in the other direction. God used His creation to bring Jonah all the way to Nineveh. In the four short chapters of Jonah's book, the wind, sea, sailors, great fish, king of Nineveh, people of Nineveh, plant, worm, and sun all obeyed God—everything except Jonah the prophet. It is amazing to see God's grace toward this struggling prophet and how His will ultimately prevails.

After Jonah accomplished his assignment to preach in Nineveh, the king and people repented of their sins. "When God saw what they did, how they turned from their evil way, God relented of the disaster that he had said he would do to them, and he did not do it" (Jonah 3:10). Jonah was so disappointed that he talked about taking his life. His expectations determined his actions, and his unmet expectations fueled his reactions. "Jonah went out of the city and sat to the east of the city and made a booth for himself there. He sat under it in the shade, till he should see what would become of the city" (Jonah 4:5). The whole book of Jonah is about a prophet who knows God, but who is dominated by strong personal expectations. Consequently, he suffers greatly because of his unmet expectations. The hero of the story is our kind, merciful, and patient God who puts up with Jonah's tantrums in a way that most people would not be willing to do.

Why are expectations such a source of pain for human beings? Let's use a scale from 1 to 10 to better explain this dynamic. Say there is going to be a special event, and you set an expectation of 8 for that event. You are hoping to have great conversations, that people are going to like you, and that people are going to love your new clothes or hairstyle. You are excited about this event, and you keep internally rehearsing your expectations, which are quite high. The event takes place, but it does not go as you had hoped. The conversations were not that great, you didn't get the impression that people liked you, no one said anything about your new clothes, and only one person commented on your new hairstyle. You are sad because you got a 2 on this event. The difference between 2 and 8 is the size of your disappointment and letdown. The Bible talks about this in Proverbs: "Hope deferred makes the heart sick…" (Prov. 13:12). Hope deferred is another term for unmet expectations. The result of a disappointment is a heartsick feeling. Many people have suffered greatly like Jonah did because of mismanaged expectations. We need to manage expectations in a healthy way. The best way to do that is to intentionally have low expectations of people and high expectations of God. People are imperfect, and, in their imperfection, they can let us down. God, on the other hand, is a perfect God. We can expect fully that God is going to be true to His promises.

I would like to share a story that a friend of mine told me. To protect his identity, we will call him Albert. When Albert was about 30 years old, he was working a 15-minute drive from where his father worked. A couple of times a month Albert would go have lunch with his father. Sometimes he would return with sadness in his heart. He knew his father loved him, but his father was immersed in his business and personal challenges and was not able to give Albert the emotional support he needed. Albert's sadness was a result of unmet expectations. He would go see his dad with a 7 in terms of expectations, and if his dad gave him a 2, the difference was the size of the disappointment Albert experienced as he drove back to work after lunch. By the way, growing up as a child Albert's father did not get much emotional support from his own father. One day, God showed Albert that he needed to pray about this in a different way. He began praying that God would meet his emotional needs in this area. If those needs were met by God, he would be able to approach his father with zero expectations. Over time, as Albert prayed like that, he found himself having lunch with his dad and driving back to work with his heart at peace. What changed? Albert's father didn't change. Albert had changed. As God was meeting those needs in his heart, he was able to lower the expectations he had of his father to zero. If Albert went to the lunch meeting expecting zero and his dad gave him a 2, that was a gain and not a loss.

I think that many times the expectations we build in our hearts are like idols. We are hoping that something will give us meaning and significance. Idols ultimately hurt us, and only God can give us meaning and significance. That is why 1 John 5:21 says, "Little children, keep yourselves from idols." We need to go to God with the needs of our hearts and not to people. "Delight yourself in the Lord, and he will give you the desires of your heart" (Ps. 37:4).

I should clarify that I am not talking here about work expectations. If you supervise a staff member, you should expect that person to work well and meet the goals that are set for them. What I am talking about in this chapter are the expectations of the heart for love, significance, support, and meaning. Those we should go to God with. He never fails. Relationships with other people will work much better if we approach them with low expectations. We should be ready to love them and to be kind to them, but at the same time not have high expectations of them.

James Dobson wrote about Stephen Hawking (1942-2018), who was an astrophysicist at Cambridge University and one of the most intelligent men on earth. He advanced the general theory of relativity farther than any person since Albert Einstein. Unfortunately, Hawking was afflicted with ALS, also known as Lou Gehrig's disease. It eventually took his life. He was confined to a wheelchair for years, where he could do little more than sit and think. Hawking even lost the ability to speak and would communicate by using a computer that was operated by the tiniest movement of his fingertips. Hawking said that before he became ill, he had very little interest in life. He called it a "pointless existence" resulting from sheer boredom. He drank too much and did very little work. Then he learned he had ALS and was not expected to live more than two years. The ultimate effect of that diagnosis, beyond its initial shock, was extremely positive. He claimed to have been happier after he was afflicted than before. How can that be understood? Hawking provided the answer: "When one's expectations are reduced to zero," he said, "one really appreciates everything that one does have." Stated another way: Contentment in life is determined in part by what a person anticipates from it. To a man like Hawking, who thought he would soon die, everything took on meaning—a sunrise, a walk in the park, or the laughter of children. Suddenly, each small pleasure became precious. By contrast, those who believe life owes them a free ride—and who have high expectations of others—are often discontent with its finest gifts.[2]

Hawking was not a Christian, but I must agree with his statement: "When one's expectations are reduced to zero, one really appreciates everything that one does have." Some of our mental battles are fueled by unmet expectations. We must address those by lowering our expectations of people and of life, in some cases, and by increasing our expectations of God, who is good and always faithful to His promises. I invite you to reflect on that unmet expectation that is the source of so much disappointment for you and to write down a prayer where you ask God to meet that need in your heart, instead of another person meeting your need. Put that paper in a visible place, and pray about it several times until God changes your heart and the unmet expectation no longer bothers you because it is now being met by God. Remember, have high expectations of God and low expectations of people. How will you lower your expectations of people and of circumstances in life? What expectation do you need to surrender to God?

Humility: How I Think of Myself

U.S. President Abraham Lincoln once became caught up in a situation where he wanted to please a politician, so he issued a command to transfer certain regiments. When his secretary of war, Edwin Stanton, received the order, Stanton refused to carry it out. He said that the president was a fool. Lincoln was told what Stanton had said, and he replied, "If Stanton said I'm a fool, then I must be, for he is nearly always right. I'll see for myself." As the two men talked, Lincoln quickly realized that his decision was a serious mistake, and without hesitation he withdrew it. Because Lincoln didn't think too highly of himself, he was able to recognize his error and correct it.[3] Most high-level leaders would rather stand by their wrong decisions instead of correcting them.

How we think about ourselves is key to avoiding and winning mental battles. As a matter of fact, thoughts of ourselves frequently occupy our minds. How should we think about ourselves? God desires for us to walk humbly before Him and before others. "He has told you, O man, what is good; and what does the Lord require of you but to do justice, and to love kindness, and to walk humbly with your God?" (Mic. 6:8). This is such a significant issue to God that He makes many promises to both the humble and the proud.

For example, "…God opposes the proud but gives grace to the humble" (1 Pet. 5:5).

Humility is directly tied to our thoughts, and it has two separate parts: how I think about myself and how I think about others. Let's consider how Christians in ministry ought to think about themselves. It is easy to have grandiose thoughts about ourselves and think that other people just don't have a clue. We look in the mirror, and we might think, "God, You are so blessed to have me on your team."

The Bible tells us how we ought to think about ourselves: "For by the grace given to me I say to everyone among you not to think of himself more highly than he ought to think, but to think with sober judgment, each according to the measure of faith that God has assigned" (Rom. 12:3). Did you hear about the minister who said he had a wonderful sermon on humility, but was waiting for a large crowd before preaching it? It's funny, but how often do we think highly of ourselves? Instead of thinking highly about myself, I need to think of myself with sober judgment. Verse 16 of the same chapter further clarifies this thought: "Never be wise in your own sight." How I think about myself will lead me to become either a prideful leader or a humble leader, and that will have a major impact on my ministry.

The Apostle Paul was a godly, powerful leader. He was not perfect, but he desired to walk humbly before God. Here's how the Apostle Paul thought of himself: "I am the least of the apostles" (1 Cor. 15:9). "I am the very least of all the saints" (Eph. 3:8). "I am the foremost of sinners" (1 Tim. 1:15). The Apostle Paul thought of himself with sober judgment. He wasn't wise in his own sight. You and I need to do the same thing.

About this topic, my former professor and friend Dr. Skip Hessel commented:

> *My career has been filled with longevity and disruption. I realize these terms would not normally go together. About the time I get comfortable in my work, God closes that door and opens another one. It takes time and energy to develop a team. I often asked, "God, why won't you allow me to see this through to completion?" Sometimes, the careers overlap on the timeline, but are very different. Trusting God fully requires a follower to face God's will with courage instead of whining inside because we cannot get our own way. I am glad God taught me humility long ago. Each time God has reset my life, He allowed me to realize achievements beyond my dreams. Then, He would reboot and start again in some way beyond my comprehension of His plan for my life. Trusting Him (Proverbs 3:5-7) was important, but understanding how He uses followers who are humble (James 4:6-7) was the greater truth as I overcame mental battles.*[4]

Sometimes we must correct other people's opinions and comments about ourselves, but we need to do so carefully. Hudson Taylor was once scheduled to speak at a large Presbyterian church in Melbourne, Australia. The moderator of the service introduced the missionary in eloquent and glowing terms. He told the large congregation all that Taylor had accomplished in China and then presented him as "our illustrious guest." Taylor stood quietly for a moment, and then opened his message by saying, "Dear friends, I am the little servant of an illustrious Master."[5] Hudson Taylor's humility was one of many character traits that made him a great leader.

A book that has a been a blessing to me over the years to help me think biblically about myself and how to have victory over the flesh is the book *Calvary Road* by Roy Hession. It is a little but mighty book. I recommend it for every Christian, especially those in ministry. This topic is critical for a Christian leader. Our ministry effectiveness is tied to our thought life. How we think about ourselves is key.

The famous inventor Samuel Morse was once asked if he ever encountered situations where he didn't know what to do. Morse responded, "More than once, and whenever I could not see my way clearly, I knelt down and prayed to God for light and understanding." Morse received many honors from his invention of the telegraph, but felt undeserving. He said, "I have made a valuable application of electricity not because I was superior to other men but solely because God, who meant it for mankind, must reveal it to someone and He was pleased to reveal it to me."[6] Samuel Morse was not wise in his own sight. We all appreciate seeing humility in others. Leaders need to be humble and think of themselves with sober judgment, not being wise in their own sight. God loves and blesses a humble heart.

Jesus had a great admiration for John the Baptist. This is what the Lord said about John: "Truly, I say to you, among those born of women there has arisen no one greater than John the Baptist..." (Matt. 11:11). Certainly, this appreciation was because of the honorable assignment that God gave John the Baptist to prepare the way for the Messiah, but I believe it was also because John was fully surrendered to the Lord. At one point John said, "He must increase, but I must decrease" (John 3:30). It is very difficult for Jesus to increase in our ministry when we are busy increasing ourselves. Humility is valued by God, and it starts in our minds. Humility will eventually translate into action, but it needs to be addressed at its origin: in our minds. Satan will place prideful thoughts in our minds. We must reject them and replace them with the truth: "He must increase, but I must decrease." Will you evaluate your thoughts and make sure you are thinking of yourself with sober judgment?

Humility: How I Think of Others

Although Anglican minister and evangelist George Whitefield disagreed with his friend and rival John Wesley on some theological matters, he was careful not to create problems in public that could be used to hinder the preaching of the Gospel. In the eighteenth century, Whitefield and brothers John and Charles Wesley founded the Methodist movement in the Church of England. When someone asked Whitefield if he thought he would see Wesley in heaven, Whitefield replied, "I fear not, for he will be so near the eternal throne and we at such a distance, we shall hardly get sight of him."[7] This is a powerful statement. Even though Whitefield had some theological disagreements with Wesley, he still thought highly of his brother in Christ. The second key area of our thought life is how we think of others. The next time you are involved in a mental battle about someone, pause to evaluate how you are thinking about that person.

As Christian leaders, how are we to think about others? In Philippians2, Paul exhorts the believers to have humility of mind by following the example of Christ's humility. "Do nothing from selfish ambition or conceit, but in humility count others more significant than yourselves. Let each of you look not only to his own interests, but also to the interests of others" (Phil. 2:3-4). In this text we are told to follow the Lord Jesus' example of humility and think of others as more significant than ourselves. That is easier said than done. Regardless of the position of a brother or sister in a church or organization, as a Christian leader I am called to think of him or her as more significant than me.

Booker T. Washington was a renowned African-American educator. Shortly after he took over the presidency of Tuskegee Institute in Alabama, he was walking in an exclusive section of town when he was stopped by a wealthy woman. Not knowing the famous Washington by sight, she asked if he would like to earn a few dollars by chopping wood for her. Because he had no pressing business at that moment, Washington smiled, rolled up his sleeves, and proceeded to do the humble chore she had requested. When he was finished, he carried the logs into the house and stacked them by the fireplace. A young girl recognized him and later revealed his identity to the lady. The next morning the embarrassed woman went to see Washington in his office at the Institute and apologized profusely. "It's perfectly all right, Madam," he replied. "Occasionally I enjoy a little manual labor. Besides, it's always a delight to do something for a friend."[8] This was one of the many reasons Washington was a great leader. He both understood humility and practiced it.

In order to win ministry mental battles, we have to think in a biblical way. We need to think of ourselves with sober judgment and not be wise in our own sight. When we think of others, we must think of them as more significant than ourselves. It is then that we experience genuine humility and follow in Christ's footsteps. This world is in desperate need of humble Christian leaders who think of themselves with sober judgment (Rom. 12:3) and who think of others as more significant than themselves (Phil. 2:3). How do I do that in practical terms? Well, how would you receive the president of your organization if he was coming to visit you? You would think of him as more significant than yourself, so you would treat him with respect and dignity. You would do special things to honor him and show your appreciation. That would be right to do, after all: You view that person as more significant than yourself. In order to follow Christ's example in this area, you must treat the cleaning person the same way that you would treat the president of the organization: as more significant than yourself.

Sometimes we desire to be humble, but we need the help of others around us who love us to help us have a more biblical view of ourselves and of others. The biblical account of Naaman illustrates the idea of those around us who care for us and desire to help us in this way. It is found in 2 Kings 5. A little captive Hebrew girl told her master's wife, "Would that my lord were with the prophet who is in Samaria! He would cure him of his leprosy" (2 Kings 5:3). Naaman was commander of the army of the king of Syria. He was a mighty man of valor, but he was a leper: a great leader with an incurable disease. This powerful leader probably tried everything to get better, but nothing worked. But the words of a little captive girl gave him hope. He ran to the king of Syria, and the king sent him to Israel with a letter to the Hebrew king.

Naaman went to the prophet Elisha's house with horses, chariots, and servants. He was a great leader who expected to be treated as such. Yet, things quickly started going downhill from Naaman's perspective. In order to receive a blessing from God, a person must be humble. "God opposes the proud but gives grace to the humble" (James 4:6). Elisha did not come to meet him; instead, he sent a messenger. I am sure that messenger was a shock to a great leader accustomed to being given preferential treatment. The instructions he heard were: "Go and wash in the Jordan seven times, and your flesh shall be restored, and you shall be clean" (2 Kings 5:10). What? Naaman responded in anger. He had expectations that he was going to be treated with great honor: "Behold, I thought that he would surely come out to me and stand and call upon the name of the Lord his God, and wave his hand over the place and cure the leper" (v. 11).

Naaman was full of expectations. As I shared earlier, great expectations can lead to great disappointment. The Jordan was a muddy river not worthy of a great leader. Naaman said, "Are not Abana and Pharpar, the rivers of Damascus, better than all the waters of Israel? Could I not wash in them and be clean?" (v. 12). Having prideful expectations can be an obstacle to humility and thus impede the blessing of God. At that point, Naaman hastily started his trip back to Syria. He was quite upset and disappointed.

His servants were the ones who convinced Naaman to humble himself and obey the word of the prophet through the messenger. "So he went down and dipped himself seven times in the Jordan, according to the word of the man of God, and his flesh was restored like the flesh of a little child, and he was clean" (v. 12). He was healed! Naaman returned joyfully to the prophet's house and confessed, "Behold, I know that there is no God in all the earth but in Israel…" (v. 15). Naaman started with a high view of himself and a low view of God's prophet. After God's miraculous work, Naaman had a low view of himself, a high view of Elisha, and an even higher view of God. We, too, must listen to those who are trying to help us have a more biblical view of ourselves and others because they see and hear us. They can counter wrong thinking with truth.

We are not the heroes. God is the hero. Everything we have comes from God: "…A person cannot receive even one thing unless it is given him from heaven" (John 3:27). Today I play a small role on the stage of life, and tomorrow I will be gone. When my parents passed away early in 2020, I began reflecting on the brevity of life. Most people know the names of their grandparents. But do you remember the names of your great-grandparents? What about their parents? If we forget the names of our family members three generations ago, that means it is likely our names will be forgotten in three generations. If that is the case, we must live our lives to lift up the only Name that truly matters: the name of Jesus Christ, the Name above all names. All other names will vanish one day. So, live your life today not striving to build yourself, your name, and your kingdom. Instead, give glory and honor to God and build His Kingdom. That is the path toward humility. Give God center stage. God will always be the main character. He will always be the hero. God will always be God, and we are but unworthy servants. Do you desire the credit that belongs to God? That is the path to pride. "Pride goes before destruction, and a haughty spirit before a fall" (Prov. 16:18).

Naaman, the powerful leader, needed the blessing of God in his life. The path to receive it was for him to learn humility as a leader. God put two people and two items in Naaman's path for him to learn humility: the captive girl, Elisha's messenger, the servants' instructions, and the Jordan River. Naaman listened and followed the voice of a little captive girl. He then obeyed the voice of the prophet's messenger. He submitted to the instructions of his servants. He then put himself under the muddy waters of the Jordan River. The picture of Naaman willingly submitting to the directives he was given is the picture that God wanted Naaman to see. It was a physical picture of a spiritual principle. Naaman needed to place himself under the mighty hand of God to receive the blessing from God. How are you doing on your journey toward humility? What or who is God using in your life to teach you humility? Are you resisting or welcoming those things or people God is using? That is the path to victory in many mental battles.

The Subtle Power of Deception

A friend of mine shared this story:

> *One of my best friends in Bible college accepted a pastorate in Louisiana. We stayed in touch weekly for years, taking turns calling each other. At first, we shared the struggles he had as a new pastor, but much to my delight he began talking about progress and victory. Later, I learned this was a deception.*
>
> *My calendar declared it was my turn to call John. I realized he had not called me the previous week. He did not answer, so I left an encouraging message. By the next week, he had not called, and I became worried. After he did not answer his personal phone, I called the church phone. The man answering my call delivered horrifying news: My dear friend was no longer pastor of the church. He would not elaborate further, so I called and called my friend's personal number to no avail. I also wrote letters. I received no answer.*
>
> *Ten years later, I was at a biblical counseling conference in Nashville, Tennessee, and recognized my long-lost friend. He bashfully acknowledged me because he was hand in hand with a woman I did not recognize as his wife. How embarrassing!*

> *We talked for almost an hour, and he explained that he fell into sin. He was already deceiving his wife and congregation, so it was easy for him to deceive me over the phone. His ministry had not gone well because he was seeking his own desires instead of God's will for him. He lost his family all at once—his church, his wife, and his children. He never dreamed he would run into me. He gave me his phone number for future contact, but he never returned my calls. A leader's desire to serve self can keep him from serving the Lord.*[9]

One of the toughest mental battles we fight is deception. Often we are able to convince ourselves that something bad for us will actually be good for us. Human beings have the capacity to be easily deceived. Thousands of years ago, God had given clear instructions that when the attack on Jericho was going to take place, the Israelites were not to take any plunder for themselves: "…keep yourselves from the things devoted to destruction, lest… you take any of the devoted things and make the camp of Israel a thing for destruction and bring trouble upon it. But all silver and gold, and every vessel of bronze and iron, are holy to the Lord; they shall go into the treasury of the Lord" (Josh. 6:18-19).

In the heat of the battle, a soldier named Achan saw some beautiful clothes and some silver and gold, and he had a mental struggle. He wanted those riches, but he knew very well the consequences promised by the Lord for keeping them for himself. In his heart he finally concluded that no one would know: It would be a secret, they would be hidden, and this would not hurt anybody. He deceived himself to the point of disobedience to God. Of course, God saw what happened, and He was not pleased.

Joshua did not know about this incident as he was preparing for the battle against the city Ai. Joshua launched the attack on the city.

Israel was defeated, and 36 Israelites were killed. The people were downcast. God spoke to Joshua and told him that this happened because "Israel has sinned." God went on to tell the people, "… thus says the Lord, God of Israel, 'There are devoted things in your midst, O Israel. You cannot stand before your enemies until you take away the devoted things from among you'" (Josh. 7:13).

God revealed that it was Achan who stole the treasure. Achan's scheme was revealed, and he confessed: "…I saw among the spoil a beautiful cloak from Shinar, and 200 shekels of silver, and a bar of gold weighing 50 shekels, then I coveted them and took them. And see, they are hidden in the earth inside my tent, with the silver underneath" (Josh. 7:21). The Israelites returned the stolen treasure to the Lord. Then Achan and his family and all his possessions were destroyed and buried under a massive pile of stones. What a sad and tragic end to what started in Achan's heart as "no one will know" and "no one will get hurt by it." In the end, everyone knew, and so many people were hurt and killed by his actions, including his own family.

Achan knew the words that had been spoken by his leader, Joshua. He knew the warning and the consequences, but he looked at the treasure and allowed his thoughts to desire and covet it. He rationalized his desires. Something he knew was bad became good for him. That is deception. Once deceived, he acted on his thoughts and emotions. As servants of the Lord, we must guard ourselves from deception. The New Testament has strong warnings against deception. For example, James reminds us: "Do not be deceived, my beloved brothers" (James 1:16). This is repeated in many other passages (1 Cor. 3:18, 6:9, and 15:33; Gal. 6:3, 7; Eph. 5:6; 2 Thess. 2:3; 1 John 3:7). The problem with deception is that you don't know you are being deceived. Your thinking is flawed, and you need external help. You cannot correct your thoughts alone. We all need the truth of God's Word to point out our wrong thinking, and we need the counsel of godly leaders to speak truth into our hearts. Perhaps you need to approach two godly leaders and invite them to feel free to speak into your life if they see anything that doesn't look right. This requires a humble attitude and an open mind to what these leaders have to say. Don't be defensive; be eager to learn. Teachability is one of the most important characteristics for a servant of God.

Both pastors and others in ministry have fallen and lost their marriages and ministries. It doesn't matter how much Bible knowledge, how many degrees, or how many years of full-time ministry experience you have: You WILL be attacked by the enemy. Satan starts messing with your thoughts as a means to start messing with your heart. God warns us to protect our hearts: "Keep your heart with all vigilance, for from it flow the springs of life" (Prov. 4:23). When your heart tells you that "no one will know" or "no one will get hurt by it," run for help! Don't believe that. It's a lie! If you choose not to seek help, that momentary pleasure can turn into destruction for you and those you love.

Christians in ministry have the interesting ability to continue to function, sometimes successfully, even though they are flirting with sin or even living in sin. In a sense they are functioning on the strengths of their gifts, and God still blesses His Word even if it is shared by dirty vessels. But that season does not last forever. We see in 2 Samuel 11 what the great King David did to Bathsheba and how he murdered her husband, Uriah. He covered his tracks the best he could, and it looked like everything was going to be OK, except for the very last sentence of the chapter: "…But the thing that David had done displeased the Lord" (2 Sam. 11:27). God saw everything that David had done, and David reaped very painful consequences.

When a ministry leader is deceived and falls into sin, the consequences can be catastrophic. Those consequences can include broken families, lost marriages, devastated churches or organizations, Christians turning from the faith, unsaved people saying they will never follow Christ, and many more. But in the moment of temptation, the consequences are kept well hidden. You never see lungs full of cancer in smoking advertising, and you don't see a drunk lying on the side of the road in alcohol advertising. The "no one will know" in the temptation could become national news on many websites and social media. Eventually, everyone will know. The enemy will steal your peace, your purity, your family, your ministry, and, in some cases, your life—if you let him.

Jim Bakker was one of the most popular televangelists in the 1980s. He and his wife, Tammy Faye, had quite a following on television. Their ministry ended with a huge scandal that included fraud and sexual abuse. In 1987, Jim's secretary publicly accused him of drugging and raping her. After Bakker resigned from the ministry, he was charged with accounting fraud and sentenced to 45 years in prison.[10] As Bakker's ministry grew, so did the finances and temptations. He did not guard his heart from deception, and he ended up thinking he could have the ministry and also behave in a worldly way. Like Achan, Jim Bakker lost everything. Bakker was not setting his mind on the things of God, but on the things of man.

Deception has much to do with Jim Bakker's journey. What mental battles did Bakker go through on his journey to end up where he did? The list of God-followers with similar journeys is quite long. We must take our mental battles with deception very seriously.

Turn to God to have victory over deception and temptation. "No temptation has overtaken you that is not common to man. God is faithful, and he will not let you be tempted beyond your ability, but with the temptation he will also provide the way of escape, that you may be able to endure it" (1 Cor. 10:13). You also must have a couple of accountability partners who know all your areas of struggle and to whom you have given permission to ask you honest accountability questions. If you don't have these key life partners, you can easily become a victim of the deception of the enemy. You don't want to find yourself isolated, facing strong temptations and thinking, like Achan, "no one will know" or "no one will get hurt by it." Will you approach a friend and give that person permission to speak into your life if they see something that doesn't look right? Will you also give that person permission to ask accountability questions?

Stewarding Authority

The U.S. Naval Institute reported this story, told by Frank Koch:

> *Two battleships assigned to the training squadron had been at sea on maneuvers in heavy weather for several days. I was serving on the lead battleship and was on watch on the bridge as night fell. The visibility was poor with patchy fog, so the captain remained on the bridge keeping an eye on all activities. Shortly after dark, the lookout on the wing reported, "Light, bearing on the starboard bow."*
>
> *"Is it steady or moving astern?" the captain called out.*
>
> *The lookout replied, "Steady, Captain," which meant we were on a dangerous collision course with that ship.*
>
> *The captain then called to the signalman, "Signal that ship: 'We are on a collision course, advise you change course twenty degrees.'"*
>
> *Back came the signal, "Advisable for you to change course twenty degrees."*
>
> *The captain said, "Send: 'I'm a captain, change course twenty degrees.'"*

> *"I'm a seaman second-class," came the reply. "You had better change course twenty degrees."*
>
> *By that time the captain was furious. He spat out, "Send: 'I'm a battleship. Change course twenty degrees.'"*
>
> *Back came the flashing light, "I'm a lighthouse."*
>
> *We changed course.*[11]

Authority disputes can be quite stressful. How leaders view their authority and how they perceive the way others view their authority can be a significant source of mental battles and subsequent problems. This chapter will address and provide suggestions for how to view your authority and the authority of other coworkers. The Bible has much to say about authority. The word authority is mentioned 97 times in the Bible, with 86 of those occurring in the New Testament.

Jesus praised a Roman centurion for his faith because he understood and exemplified the concept of authority. Jesus arrived at Capernaum, and the centurion came to speak to Him. He said, "Lord, my servant is lying paralyzed at home, suffering terribly" (Matt. 8:6). Jesus felt compassion for both the centurion and his servant and said, "I will come and heal him" (Matt. 8:7). Most people would have thanked Jesus and asked him to follow them to the place where the ministry was needed. "But the centurion replied, 'Lord, I am not worthy to have you come under my roof, but only say the word, and my servant will be healed" (Matt. 8:8). With these words the centurion revealed a deep understanding of faith. But he continued, "For I too am a man under authority, with soldiers under me. And I say to one, 'Go,' and he goes, and to another, 'Come,' and he comes, and to my servant, 'Do this,' and he does it" (Matt. 8:9). With this comment the centurion revealed that he understood how authority works, that he recognized Jesus' divine authority, and that he was willing to trust Christ's authority. Jesus was very impressed. "When Jesus heard this, he marveled and said to those who followed him, 'Truly, I tell you, with no one in Israel have I found such faith'" (Matt. 8:10). He made a few more comments about the faith of the Gentiles and of the Hebrews, then turned to the centurion and said, "Go; let it be done for you as you have believed." And the servant was healed at that very moment (Matt. 8:13).

What made this centurion a great leader was a deep understanding of faith and authority. The centurion believed in God and recognized Him as the authority over all things: a divine authority to be followed and obeyed by faith. Most ministry leaders have studied the topic of biblical authority in the Scriptures, but sometimes in the middle of mental and ministry battles their thinking on this topic gets confused. I believe that leaders in ministry today will excel in their ministry and experience greater peace when they add a growing understanding of the biblical principles of authority to their faith in Christ. Authority is influence. Most people have a measure of influence in their lives: teachers, pastors, police officers, department supervisors, parents, etc. Let's consider some principles that will help us gain a deeper understanding of authority.

All leaders, secular or religious, get their authority from God.

All authority has divine origin, even though that authority can be used by humans for evil purposes. When Pilate asked Jesus, "Do you not know that I have authority to release you and authority to crucify you?" Jesus answered him, "You would have no authority over me at all unless it had been given you from above..." (John 19:10-11). Because the authority is not ours, we must handle it with much care and humility. "For there is no authority except from God, and those that exist have been instituted by God" (Rom. 13:1). This principle is very important. I have seen leaders behave like their authority is their own. The proof of that is when they become flustered when anyone questions their authority. In their minds, they earned the degrees, the promotions, the titles, etc., so "their" authority belongs to them. Not so. It is God's authority, not ours. The same God who gave us the ministry assignment and the authority that goes with it can take it away if we are not good stewards of it. "God removes kings and sets up kings" (Dan. 2:21). By the way, every time we remind people of our title to get things to go our way, we are earthly minded and are displaying weak leadership, as in the following case.

Christian Herter was governor of Massachusetts from 1953 to 1957 and decided to run for a second term in office. One day, after a busy morning chasing votes and no lunch, he arrived at a church barbecue. It was late afternoon, and Herter was famished. As Herter moved down the serving line, he held out his plate to the woman serving chicken. She put a piece on his plate and turned to the next person in line.

"Excuse me," Governor Herter said, "do you mind if I have another piece of chicken?"

"Sorry," the woman told him, "I'm supposed to give one piece of chicken to each person."

"But I'm starved," the governor said.

"Sorry," the woman said again. "Only one to a customer."

Governor Herter was a modest and unassuming man, but he decided that this time he would throw a little weight around. "Do you know who I am?" he said. "I am the governor of this state."

"Do you know who I am?" the woman said. "I'm the lady in charge of the chicken. Move along, mister."[12]

Ministry leaders serve under the authority of God.

The measure of authority given to us when we received our ministry assignment came from God and continues to belong to Him. It is not that it came from God and is now ours. It is not our authority; it has always belonged to God. That means that we serve under His authority. This is a very important principle that impacts our stewardship of that authority. We actually serve in submission to God's authority. Jesus, who ministered with divine authority, talked about His submission to the Father: "When you have lifted up the Son of Man, then you will know that I am he, and that I do nothing on my own authority, but speak just as the Father taught me" (John 8:28). Knowing that authority comes from God, belongs to God, and is in submission to Him will set us free to not fight for our authority, because it was never ours. We don't have to be defensive: God defends and protects what belongs to Him. We don't have to be upset in the flesh when our authority is questioned. God's divine authority is not stewarded by our flesh, but by faith. For us to impress God like the centurion impressed Jesus, we need to have a deep understanding of faith and authority. Hold your authority with an open hand. God put it there, and God can take it away if you don't steward it correctly or if He has other plans for you. Don't fear losing authority It is not yours anyway. If you fear losing authority, you are grasping it too tightly. When you do that, it slips from your hand. The best way to keep your authority is to keep a loose grip on it. Let God do the holding.

Some leaders get very defensive with the authority they were given to steward. Any little thing feels like a threat to them. They feel when their authority is shaken, their whole being and identity are shaken. In cases like this, leaders need to check their self-esteem. Feeling threatened could be a sign that a leader has low self-esteem and is leaning on position, title, and authority for significance. This is wrong thinking and is a form of idolatry. Leaders need to go to the Lord to develop healthy self-esteem. What God thinks of us must be the basis of our significance. Leaders need to learn to be secure and confident in themselves, based on God's promises and the value God places on each person.

I remember a time when a pastor felt like his authority was being questioned, and he said, "I am the anointed of the Lord; you can't do this to me. I am right; you are not." He was feeling like his authority was being checked and was grasping at something, some kind of lifesaver. When leaders are confident in the Lord, they will not be shaken when others seem to question their leadership. The fear of God overcomes the fear of men.

Authority can be misused to hurt others.

We see this in the life of Saul when he used his authority to persecute Christians. "And I did so in Jerusalem. I not only locked up many of the saints in prison after receiving authority from the chief priests, but when they were put to death I cast my vote against them" (Acts 26:10). I am tired of the regular news of Christian leaders who have used their authority for evil. Pastors and other ministry leaders are accused of abusing children or women or of misusing money and abusing power. We must keep our hearts in check. Long before the acts took place, those leaders were allowing their hearts to stray. Mental battles were lost. Leaders were having inappropriate thoughts, but they did not remove the thoughts, did not seek godly counsel, and entertained those thoughts in the privacy of their minds.

Over time, wrong thinking leads to strong emotions, which can lead to wrong decisions. The temptations are real and strong. The enemy promises that no one will know and that no one will get hurt—until the day comes when everyone knows and everyone is hurt. Then leaders lose their ministries and, many times, their families. They were given authority, but they ended up using it to hurt people. If you are somewhere in that progression, run for help! Leave the lonely, dark corner where your mental battle is taking place and run to the light. Ask for help. Talk to the leaders in your ministry. Get a biblical counselor to help you. Find a couple of accountability partners to lead you on a journey from your personal darkness to the light of Christ that cleanses all things and restores relationships. "But if we walk in the light, as he is in the light, we have fellowship with one another, and the blood of Jesus his Son cleanses us from all sin" (1 John 1:7).

Authority must be used to build up others.

God's power of redemption is amazing. Once Saul came to faith in Christ, he stopped using his Hebrew name and started using his Roman name, Paul, and he began to use his authority to bless people. "For even if I boast a little too much of our authority, which the Lord gave for building you up and not for destroying you, I will not be ashamed" (2 Cor. 10:8). I would say this is the only reason God entrusts anyone with a measure of authority. It is not to build your name and your social media following; it is to build people up. That is the work of the Holy Spirit. God invites us to come along and join Him in that work. Authority is not about building your kingdom, but about building God's Kingdom.

Remember Diotrephes? "I have written something to the church, but Diotrephes, who likes to put himself first, does not acknowledge our authority. So if I come, I will bring up what he is doing, talking wicked nonsense against us. And not content with that, he refuses to welcome the brothers, and also stops those who want to and puts them out of the church" (3 John 1:9-10). Don't be a Diotrephes. Ministry is not about the ministry leader.

I have seen ministry leaders taking on a savior mentality. They think that if things are not done their way, the ministry is lost. So, they use their authority to fight hard for theirway. In the process they do great damage to the body of Christ. God calls us to serve Him and gives us a measure of authority so we can bless people and glorify God. Anything beyond that is the flesh, the world, and the devil getting into the mix and warping God's design. Tragedy is the most likely result. Things might go well for a season, but it is only a matter of time until our little kingdom comes tumbling down. At times we can go from stewarding Christ's authority to imposing our own. God's Word has a warning for us to avoid that: "The one who speaks on his own authority seeks his own glory; but the one who seeks the glory of him who sent him is true, and in him there is no falsehood" (John 7:18).

Ministry leaders are stewards of the Lord's authority.

At the end of His earthly ministry, the Jesus said, "All authority in heaven and on earth has been given to me. Go therefore and make disciples of all nations, baptizing them in the name of the Father and of the Son and of the Holy Spirit, teaching them to observe all that I have commanded you. And behold, I am with you always, to the end of the age" (Matt. 28:18-20). There is something so powerful about these words, which are called the Great Commission. All authority belongs to Christ. Not some authority, but all authority, including what you think is yours. After Jesus made that statement, He said in an authoritative way, "Go!" That's it. He was giving authority to His disciples to serve His purposes: making disciples, baptizing, and teaching obedience to the things Christ had commanded the disciples. They went. The result was that the Gospel circled the globe, and one day it arrived to you and me. The commission worked!

As believers and ministry leaders, we "go" under Christ's authority. He sends us out as stewards of His authority to serve Him and accomplish His purposes. Jesus taught a parable to explain stewardship of the talents that God provides. In Matthew 25:14-30 The Master provided talents, or wealth, but He expected them to be well stewarded. Those who did so heard the words, "Well done, good and faithful servant. You have been faithful over a little; I will set you over much. Enter into the joy of your master" (Matt. 25:23). The servant who did not steward the Master's talent heard words of rebuke and judgment. Jesus concluded this parable with the application: "For to everyone who has will more be given, and he will have an abundance. But from the one who has not, even what he has will be taken away" (Matt. 25:29).

God seems to reward good stewardship of what He provides. In Matthew 25, He rewarded good stewardship of authority with more of it and rewarded bad stewardship of authority by removing it. Have you seen this happen? Perhaps the area ministry director who managed authority in a godly way was given more authority by being asked to oversee a larger area. In another parable Jesus specifically referred to authority as the reward: "And he said to him, 'Well done, good servant! Because you have been faithful in a very little, you shall have authority over ten cities" (Luke 19:17).

The next time you are in a meeting where authority tension will arise, ask a close friend in the meeting to listen carefully to what you say and to talk to you afterward about it. You want to make sure you are being a good steward of authority and not mishandling it. Your words reveal your heart. Accept constructive criticism. Authority disputes and management are sources of many mental battles. Leaders need to remember that they are not the owners of the authority they have. They are stewards of God's authority entrusted to them. That authority must be used to build people up, not for selfish purposes. One day we will give account of how we managed God's authority assigned to us. Because of that, we must lead with humility. How are you stewarding the authority God has entrusted to you?

God's Antidote for Fear

When businessman Allan C. Emery was in the wool business, he once spent an evening with a shepherd on the Texas prairie. During the night, the long wail of coyotes pierced the air. The shepherd's dogs growled and peered into the darkness. The sheep, which had been sleeping, lumbered to their feet, alarmed, bleating pitifully. The shepherd tossed more logs onto the fire, and the flames shot up. In the glow, Allan looked out and saw thousands of little lights. He realized those were reflections of the fire in the eyes of the sheep. "In the midst of danger," he observed, "the sheep were not looking out into the darkness but were keeping their eyes set in the direction of their safety, looking toward the shepherd. They are comforted by the presence of their shepherd. I couldn't help but think of Hebrews 12: 'looking unto Jesus, the author and finisher of our faith…'"[13] In the presence of the Shepherd of our lives, we will experience protection from fearful things.

Human beings have a problem with fear. Our hearts are prone to fear. We are fearful by nature. There are so many things in life that can trigger fear in our hearts. We fear the future, we fear bad things that might happen—we even fear fear itself. God knows we have a problem with fear, and more than 100 times in the Bible He says, "fear not" or "do not fear." Ministry leaders are not exempt from this fear problem. They need to learn to control their fears, or mental battles will be sparked by those fears. I have had many mental battles fueled by fear. I can testify of the negative impact fear can have on life, ministry, and ministry decisions.

What is fear? Fear is apprehension, trepidation, dread, fright, panic, or terror. Our hearts can easily be filled with fear. Here are some of the many things we fear: the unknown, the unfamiliar, unemployment, economic instability, isolation, loss of health, war, social decay, being dependent, spiders, snakes, earthquakes, broken relationships, disapproval, what others think, rejection, strangers, abandonment, being ridiculed, loneliness, failure, being out of control, loss of security, insignificance, and much more.

Fear is a root cause of many other problems, such as discouragement, doubt, worry, and anxiety. God has made provision for us not to be defeated by fear. A few years ago, my heart was wrestling with fear. One day God brought me to a "fear not" Bible verse. Isaiah 41:10 says, "Fear not, for I am with you; be not dismayed, for I am your God; I will strengthen you, I will help you, I will uphold you with my righteous right hand."

As I meditated upon this Bible verse, God began to encourage my heart. There are three powerful truths in this verse that help us focus on Him and achieve victory over fear.

Fear and the presence of God

First, we should not fear because God says, "I am with you." You would have no fear if a strong bodyguard was with you as you walked around the city. Here's good news: God, the Creator of the universe, the most powerful being ever, is with you all the time:

"Christ in you the hope of glory" (Col. 1:27). That truth helps calm our fears.

The Lord Jesus finished the Great Commission with the words, "I am with you always, to the end of the age" (Matt. 28:20). Our problem is that we forget that God is with us. We focus so much on the problem at hand that we forget God is present with us. We have a memory problem. Fear comes when we forget He is present and fail to focus on that truth. Do you remember Peter walking on water? He succeeded as long as his eyes were fixed on the present Christ. Once his focus shifted from Jesus to the circumstances, the wind and waves, he began to sink. He quickly focused his attention on Jesus and was rescued. I think we have a memory and focus problem when it comes to the truth of the presence of God in our lives. God's presence is the antidote to fear—we just need to hold on to it.

Victory over fear comes from the presence of God. He is always with us. There is nowhere in the entire universe, on land or sea, in heaven or in hell, where one can flee from God's presence. "Am I a God at hand, declares the Lord, and not a God far away? Can a man hide himself in secret places so that I cannot see him? declares the Lord. Do I not fill heaven and earth? declares the Lord" (Jer. 23:23-24). The psalmist wrote, "Where shall I go from your Spirit? Or where shall I flee from your presence? If I ascend to heaven, you are there! If I make my bed in Sheol, you are there! If I take the wings of the morning and dwell in the uttermost parts of the sea, even there your hand shall lead me, and your right hand shall hold me" (Ps. 139:7-10). God's presence is constant.

Benefits and blessings of the presence of God

Joy: "You make known to me the path of life; in your presence there is fullness of joy; at your right hand are pleasures forevermore" (Ps. 16:11).

Guidance and rest: "And he said, "My presence will go with you, and I will give you rest" (Ex. 33:14).

Freedom: "Now the Lord is the Spirit, and where the Spirit of the Lord is, there is freedom" (2 Cor. 3:17).

Protection: "In the cover of your presence you hide them from the plots of men" (Ps. 31:20).

The early American Indians had a unique practice of training young braves. After learning hunting, scouting, and fishing skills, on the night of a boy's 13th birthday, he was put to one final test. He was placed in a dense forest to spend the entire night alone. Until then, he had never been away from the security of the family and tribe. But on this night, he was blindfolded and taken several miles away. When he took off the blindfold, he was in the middle of thick woods, and he was terrified. Every time a twig snapped, he visualized a wild animal ready to pounce. After what seemed like an eternity, dawn broke, and the first rays of sunlight entered the interior of the forest. Looking around, the boy saw flowers, trees, and the outline of a path. Then, to his utter astonishment, he beheld the figure of a man standing just a few feet away, armed with bow and arrow. It was his father. He had been there all night. If that young man had realized that his dad was right next to him, he would have been relaxed all night.[14] Let's remember that continual reflection on the constant presence of God with us will help diminish our fears.

Fear and the power of God

Second, we should not fear because of who God is:"for I am your God" (Isa. 41:10). As we meditate on the character of God—for example, His power—we quickly realize that He is much bigger than the person or thing that is triggering fear in our hearts. "So we can confidently say, 'The Lord is my helper; I will not fear; what can man do to me?'" (Heb. 13:6). The Bible invites us not to fear men, but to fear God. The more we focus on God and learn to fear Him, the less we will fear men.

We must fear God because of who He is. In some places in the Bible, God says for us not to fear. In other places it tells us that we must fear God instead of fearing people, things, and the future. We ought to fear God. The more we learn about God, the more we will fear God, which is a good thing according to the Scripture: "Praise the Lord! Blessed is the man who fears the Lord, who greatly delights in his commandments!" (Ps. 112:1).

English author and clergyman William Gurnall said, "We fear men so much because we fear God so little."[15] If we are going to fear people less, we need to learn to fear God more. What does the fear of God mean? Does it mean we ought to be scared of God? Yes and no. The most fearful thing in a Christian's life should be the displeasure of God. American Presbyterian clergyman William Anderson said, "The fear of God is reverential trust and hatred of evil."[16] Of course, true fear of God also involves true love. Therefore, the most desired thing in a Christian's life should be the smile of God. We need to live and walk in the fear of God, living our lives in a way that we demonstrate that we care about what God thinks about our thoughts and actions. Evangelical theologian and author Wayne Grudem wrote, "The fear of God is the desire to avoid God's displeasure and discipline on our lives."[17]

The fear of God also includes a sense of awe, deep respect, and admiration. If you take a trip to see Niagara Falls, you can ride on the Maid of the Mist boat tour right out into the basin of the falls. You can walk down the steps to the edge of the bottom of the falls. You can go into the caves behind the falls where openings have been cut out. It is a terrifying thing to stand only inches from such power and from possible death, deafened by a thunderous roar, with the ground trembling from six million cubic feet of water bursting over the falls every minute, falling nearly 170 feet into the basin below. This reminds me of the fear of God. It isn't an unhealthy fear, but an overwhelming sense of awe of God Himself. If we feel a kind of fear and awe over a mere waterfall, how much more should we feel about the Lord God, who is unimaginably more powerful than a waterfall.

There are different degrees of fear. The fear of God is the highest form of fear. Our greater fear should be God, not men. The fear of God will lead us into the path of righteousness. Proverbs 29:25a says, "The fear of man lays a snare…." There is an inscription in London's Westminster Abbey to John Laird Mair, the first Lord Lawrence, that says, "He feared Man so little, because he feared God so much."[18] When God is our greatest fear, all other fears are greatly diminished. I love how the Bible describes Job as a man who feared God: "There was a man in the land of Uz whose name was Job, and that man was blameless and upright, one who feared God and turned away from evil" (Job 1:1). Because Job feared God, he turned away from evil and was righteous.

If you are going to overcome your fears, you need to decide who you are going to fear. Are you going to fear God—or man? Are you going to fear the God who controls the future—or fear the future? The person who fears men and things occupies his thoughts with the things he fears and many times can hardly sleep, consumed with fear and worry. In contrast, during World War II, an elderly woman in England had endured the nerve-shattering bombings with amazing serenity. When asked to give the secret of her calmness amid the terror and danger, she replied, "Well, every night I say my prayers. And then I remember that God is always watching, so I go peacefully to sleep. After all, there is no need for both of us to stay awake!"[19] As you focus on God and who He is, fear dissipates. The more you fear God, the less you fear other things or people.

Fear and the promises of God

Finally, Isaiah 41:10 tells us, "…I will strengthen you, I will help you, I will uphold you with my righteous right hand." We should not fear because of what He does or what He promises to do. Do you need strength and help to tackle the issue that is causing fear? He will give it to you. The God who upholds the universe is upholding you (Heb. 1:3; Ps. 63:8).

If fear is left unchecked, it can paralyze and shackle us. American comedian and counselor Michael Pritchard cleverly said, "Fear is that little darkroom where negatives are developed."[20] Let's take a look at the three promises in the last portion of Isaiah 41:10.

I will strengthen you. When your heart is gripped by fear, you feel powerless and without strength. God says: "Don't fear; I will strengthen you." For God, nothing is impossible! He has unlimited strength and can strengthen you even in the midst of difficult circumstances. Abraham was an older man when he heard that his nephew Lot had been taken captive by a military force made up of the combined armies of five kings (Gen. 14). Abraham could have been paralyzed by fear. Instead, he gathered his men together, a much smaller force, and they pursued the large army by trusting the strength of the Lord. Abraham defeated them and brought back his nephew, Lot, and many others who had been taken captive. In the situations of life that give you fear, God says, "I will strengthen you with my righteous right hand."

I will help you. When your heart is gripped by fear, you feel helpless. God says: "Don't fear; I will help you." Hebrews 13:6 says, "So we can confidently say, 'The Lord is my helper… I will not fear; what can man do to me?'" Sometimes God's help is unseen, and sometimes it is miraculous. Either way, God is always there to help. Do you believe Him?

John Paton became a missionary to the islands of the South Pacific in the late 1800s. While there, he had many scary moments such as this time:

> *[A]bout ten o'clock Mr. Paton was awakened from sleep by his little dog, Clutha. He awoke the Mathiesons, and as they watched from within the house, they saw a company of savages with flaming torches set fire to the church, and then to the reed fence that connected the church and house. A few moments more, and the house would be on fire, while armed men waited ready to kill the missionaries as soon as they tried to escape.*
>
> *With a small American tomahawk in hand, Mr. Paton ran out, cut the fence, and threw it into the flames. Seeing shadows on the ground,*

> *he looked up, finding himself surrounded by seven or eight savages, with their huge clubs raised. "Kill him! Kill him!" they shouted. Mr. Paton said, "Dare to strike me, and my Jehovah God will punish you. He protects us, and will punish you for burning His church, for hatred to His worship and people, and for all your bad conduct. We love you all; and only for doing you good you want to kill us. But our God is here now to protect us and to punish you."*
>
> *They yelled in savage hate, but no one seemed willing to strike the first blow. Just at that moment an awful tornado of wind and rain was heard coming from the south. If it had come from the north, the flames from the burning church would have reached the house and it would surely have been destroyed. But the wind blew the flames away from the house, and soon a torrent of rain was falling. The natives terror-stricken said, "That is Jehovah's rain! Truly their Jehovah is fighting for them and helping them. Let us away!" Soon every one of them had gone and Mr. Paton went to the mission-house. As he entered, Mr. Mathieson exclaimed, "If ever, in time of need, God sent help and protection to His servants in answer to prayer, He has done so tonight! Blessed be His holy name!"*[21]

Just as He helped these South Pacific missionaries and countless others, God promises to help you with the challenges you face in your life.

I will uphold you. Sometimes you go through seasons of life that are scary, and you feel out of control and at the mercy of the winds of circumstance. In the situations of life that give us fear, God tells us not to fear, as He will uphold us with his righteous right hand. The reference to God's righteous right hand is a reference to His power as seen in the creation of heavens and the earth. "My hand laid the foundation of the earth, and my right hand spread out the heavens…" (Isa. 48:13).

God through His Son upholds the universe. "He is the radiance of the glory of God and the exact imprint of his nature, and he upholds the universe by the word of his power. After making purification for sins, he sat down at the right hand of the Majesty on high" (Heb. 1:3). The truth that God upholds the universe is comforting. We are not left to randomness. There is another truth that takes this idea to a very personal level: God upholds *you*. "My soul clings to you; your right hand upholds me" (Ps. 63:8). This is a powerful thought. The same loving hand of God that upholds the universe is upholding you.

There was a study done in 2008 near Greenland concerning the movement of icebergs. Scientists noticed that smaller icebergs were moved around by winds and by water drag. They also noticed that the larger icebergs were carried around by wind and water drag, but especially by ocean currents. These movements can cause a person to see a smaller iceberg moving in one direction carried by the wind and a larger iceberg moving in a different direction carried by an ocean current. This can illustrate our lives when we face difficulties. We, too, are moved by two different forces. The surface winds in our lives can be situations that we did not plan, difficult circumstances that come upon us and cause significant stress. However, at the same time, there is another even more powerful current at work: the powerful movement of God's sovereign work ensuring that His eternal purposes are fulfilled while He carries us with His loving embrace.

Remembering who this God is will help as you face the stresses of life.

+ + +

A staff member from my ministry office in Portland, Oregon, told me that some time back they were under attack by atheists who disliked the fact that our mission agency was teaching the Bible in public schools. As those who sought to bring harm to the ministry continued these attacks, they went to the media, they went to the schools and superintendents, and they did everything they could do with children as their pawns. All this took a toll on the local director. He carried a heavy burden as he led the local ministry at that time. In human terms, this could result in a very negative impact on the ministry and, ultimately, on the boys and girls we served, as our Bible Clubs could close in Portland and potentially throughout the United States. However, the local director was also the first to lead the team in prayer and the first to put confidence in God to do His will in protecting and blessing the ministry. As each challenge came along, the director was a calming force. He chose to lead the staff and volunteers away from dramatic and rash responses in favor of trusting God to do His work. Even though they talked about some very human responses and emotions evoked from their work, every response was intentional and covered well in prayer. Eventually, they were able to see how God used even the tactics of the enemy to grow the ministry: New clubs started, and the publicity actually brought more children to clubs. Meanwhile, the opposing clubs that intended to drive a wedge in the community quickly faltered and faded away, never gaining footing past the one family that attended a few times before the club folded.[22]

Isaiah 41:10 is a rich verse that contains five promises you can focus on and believe in. Perhaps you can write these promises down and put them on your bathroom mirror:

> God, I believe:
>
> 1. You are with me.
> 2. You are my God.
> 3. You will strengthen me.
> 4. You will help me.
> 5. You will uphold me.
>
> God never fails on His promises. These are solid promises to hold on to.

Pray through Isaiah 41:10. Pray through these truths. Allow the truth of God's Word to deliver you from the bondage of fear. Don't allow fear to take up residence in your heart because of where God is (with you), because of who He is, and because of what He does. "And you will know the truth, and the truth will set you free" (John 8:32). Do you have some fears that need to be pushed out of your mind and your heart by the truth of God's Word? God's will for us is encapsulated in the words the angel of the Lord spoke to Daniel: "And he said, 'O man greatly loved, fear not, peace be with you; be strong and of good courage'" (Dan. 10:19). Ask God to remove fear from your heart and to give you strength and courage.

Over the years, Isaiah 41:10 has become a place of refuge for seasons of fear: "Fear not, for I am with you; be not dismayed, for I am your God; I will strengthen you, I will help you, I will uphold you with my righteous right hand." Time and time again God has used the truths of this verse to defeat fear in my heart. The presence, power, and promises of God can help us have victory over fear. How will you use Isaiah 41:10 to help you have victory over fear?

Our Future and God's Presence

Joseph Copeland served alongside John Paton, mentioned earlier, in mission work in the South Pacific islands. "Almost everyone thought it very strange and very foolish for two young men to give their lives for the salvation of people so cruel and uncivilized as the natives of the South Pacific islands. One old gentleman said, 'The cannibals! you will be eaten by the cannibals!' Mr. Paton said, 'Mr. Dickson, you are advanced in years now, and your own prospect is: soon to be laid in the grave, there to be eaten by worms; and I confess to you, that if I can live and die serving and honoring the Lord Jesus, it will make no difference to me whether I am eaten by cannibals or by worms; and in the Great Day my resurrection body will arise as fair as yours in the likeness of our risen Redeemer.' The old gentleman had nothing more to say."[23]

Humans are inclined to be fearful about the future. What are we going to encounter around the corner? What will the future look like? If we are honest with ourselves, we have spent many hours during the day and in the middle of the night worried about the future, anxious about something that is going to happen in the future. Most of the situations we worry about in the future never come to pass. Nevertheless, we worry about the future. Our mind and our imagination create a factory of worry about future circumstances.

This worry about the future stirs many mental battles in people. People in ministry are not immune to this. I remember when I was a student in the Portuguese Bible Institute in the early1980s. I woke up one night with thoughts racing. I had a knot in my stomach. Not feeling well, I got up and walked around the dorm. One of my friends had several apples on a plate. I thought that I would eat an apple to get rid of that weird feeling in my stomach. It didn't work. I ate all the apples (maybe five), and still no improvement. Then I realized that the knot in my stomach was worry. I was going to get married eight months later. I had no money, I needed to find an apartment to rent, and I needed to get furniture. My mind was swirling with all the things that needed to happen, and I had no clue how they could happen. I couldn't sleep and had a knot in my stomach not because I was hungry, but because I was being consumed with worry. When I now look back on the decades that I have been married to Maryjane, I confess that God was there during the whole journey, and He met all our needs. That worry was an exercise in futility. I wish I could say I never worried about future things since that time, yet the opposite is true. There have been many times of worry about the future. I think this is a mental battle we will fight many times.

Does God offer a solution for our fear and worry about the future? Does he offer a solution for our worry about future meetings, conversations, diagnoses, finances, etc.? Yes. He reminds us time and time again that His presence is the antidote for our concerns about the future. God wants us to acknowledge His presence every day, every moment of the day. We tend to lose sight of it so easily. Let's consider an example of a servant of God who was told to remember the presence of God. After the death of Moses, God asked Joshua to be the new leader of Israel. Joshua knew the task was not going to be easy, and he was obviously struggling with fear. Joshua's worry about the future was understandable. He had to lead that stubborn people, he and the people had to cross the Jordan River, he had to fight many battles, and he had to occupy land. The task was enormous. Perhaps you feel the same way. There may be several challenges in front of you that you worry about, and that can cause fear in your heart. Some people live with worry and fear 24/7.

God presented a solution to Joshua's concern for the future. In the first nine verses of the book of Joshua, God tells His servant Joshua many important truths. I would like to highlight one truth that God repeated twice as the solution to Joshua's fear. Here's the first time it is mentioned: "No man shall be able to stand before you all the days of your life. Just as I was with Moses, so I will be with you. I will not leave you or forsake you" (Josh. 1:5). The Lord promised to Joshua that He would be with him, and He would not leave him.

God ends His talk to Joshua by emphasizing once more His presence: "…Do not be frightened, and do not be dismayed, for the Lord your God is with you wherever you go" (Josh. 1:9). In these words, God clearly states that fear and worry about future situations are defeated by the presence of God. That is an incredible statement made by the Lord. The presence of God is the antidote to fear. Hallelujah!

There is only one question left. How does one use this antidote? We are not Old Testament believers; during that time, the Spirit of God would come and go from God's servants. We are New

Testament believers. When we trusted Christ as our Savior, the Holy Spirit came to dwell in us permanently. Our bodies are temples of the Holy Spirit. If we have God in us permanently, why, then, do we experience so much worry and fear? I certainly have had many seasons of experiencing fear, worry, and anxiety about the future.

John 17 is a key chapter in understanding how we as Christians can live victoriously in this world. In this chapter, Jesus prays for us to succeed in the world. In verse 17 he prays, "Sanctify them in the truth; your word is truth" (John 17:17). "Sanctify" means to separate from things profane and dedicate to God. Worry and fear belong to the world; they are not of God. As we live in the world, worry and fear attach to our minds. There is only one thing that can remove those worldly thoughts: the truth of God's Word. How then do we apply the truth of God's Word about the presence of God to defeat worry and fear?

Before we answer that question, we need to realize that our mind has the capacity to time travel. This ability to think ahead allows us to plan a vacation or a ministry event. One thing we must remember about thinking about the future is that when we are thinking ahead, we don't have God's grace to live in it. When tomorrow becomes today, then God gives sufficient grace for it. When you begin to live in the future through your mind, without the grace of God, we can crumble under its weight. The result is worry and fear. The Lord Jesus said, "Therefore, do not be anxious about tomorrow, for tomorrow will be anxious for itself. Sufficient for the day is its own trouble" (Matt. 6:34).

A good way to apply the truth of God's presence to defeat worry and fear is to do the following: When your mind begins thinking about something in the future, you should pray, "Thank you, God, that you will be there with me." Or you can say, "Thank you, God, that you will be there with me and give me the words to talk to that person." Or even: "Thank you, God, that you will be there with me and give me the wisdom to make the right decision." Do that every time you begin to think about something in the future, whether it will happen one day later, one month later, or longer. You will begin to experience less worry as you find yourself "cast[ing] all your anxieties on him, because he cares for you" (1 Pet. 5:7).

A good way to illustrate the tension of knowing God is present, but not focusing on His presence is found in the previously mentioned story of Peter walking on water in Matthew 14:22-33. While Peter focused on the presence of Jesus, he rose above his difficult and scary circumstances. Peter walked on water toward Jesus. But when his focus changed from Jesus to the circumstances, the problems began to overcome him: "But when he saw the wind, he was afraid, and beginning to sink..." (v. 30). Then Peter changed his focus back to Jesus and cried out, "Lord, save me." Jesus reached down to him and "took hold of him." Peter, once again, was no longer weighed down by his circumstances. This back-and-forth describes our lives well. So many times, the Lord is right there with us, but we do not acknowledge that, and our focus is on our problems. Suddenly we find ourselves overcome by those problems. We must learn how to focus on the presence of God.

The act of affirming the truth of God's presence is like a breath of fresh air, a wave of biblical truth that sweeps through our mind and begins to remove the worldly fear and worry. The result of this exercise with God's truth will be growing peace in our hearts. The Lord Jesus said, "I have said these things to you, that in me you may have peace. In the world you will have tribulation. But take heart; I have overcome the world" (John 16:33). How will you bring the truth of God's presence to your thinking and to your planning for future events?

Patience: Waiting a Long Time Before Expressing Anger

In 1993 we were living in Portugal. My wife was expecting our third child, a daughter. At the time the Portuguese hospitals did not allow husbands to be present in the delivery room, but Maryjane really wanted me to be there. We found out about a private hospital in Lisbon that would allow me in the delivery room to be with Maryjane and began the process of applying to go there for the delivery. We were denied because we could not get the necessary insurance, as she was expecting already. This gave us much sadness. Why did God close this door on us? This was an upsetting disappointment. Months later Rebeca was born in the large Lisbon state maternity. To our surprise, she was born with dangerously low platelets and was rushed to intensive care. There she received the care she needed, and Maryjane was able to stay at the hospital those five days and be with her. Later we realized that God was displaying His goodness all along by closing the door for the private hospital. That hospital did not have neonatal intensive care. If Rebeca had been born there, she would have had to be rushed by ambulance to the Lisbon maternity. On top of that, Maryjane would not have been able to be with her those five days. God knew all this. God knew that that earlier closed door meant saving baby Rebeca's life. When we realized that, we asked God forgiveness for our lack of patience and lack of trusting Him, and we praised Him for His mercy, grace, and goodness.

Patience is not an easy skill. Lack of patience tends to intensify mental battles. Many people involved in ministry experience great turmoil and lack of peace because they fail to wait on the Lord for His work to get accomplished. They are quick to take matters into their own hands, which often results in more problems. Or they are quick to throw in the towel. The concept of patience gets a bad reputation in Christian circles. People in general don't like to wait, so they don't like the idea of patience because they think it just means waiting. Some Christians say that you should not pray for patience because God will send you trials for you to learn patience. It seems that patience is this negative quality that we need to stay away from. However, the concept of biblical patience is much deeper and richer than this.

There are two key Greek words in the New Testament translated into the English word "patience." The first word is *makrothumia* from the Greek roots *makros* (long) and *thymos* (passion or anger). This word has the idea of waiting a long time before expressing anger, and the concept of waiting a long time before expressing anger is a characteristic of God. *Makrothumia* is used of God Himself several times in the Bible. For example, God does not desire people to perish and patiently waits for them to turn to Him: "The Lord… is patient toward you, not wishing that any should perish, but that all should reach repentance" (2 Pet. 3:9). The patience of the Lord results in the salvation of souls. "And count the patience of our Lord as salvation…" (2 Pet. 3:15). All the Bible verses in 2 Peter 3 use the Greek word *makrothumia.*

A beautiful example of this patience of God was displayed while Noah's ark was being built. The God who created the universe in six days waited nearly 75 years for Noah to build the ark. We know God could have spoken the ark into existence, so why wait 75 years? The Apostle Peter wrote, "…God's patience waited in the days of Noah, while the ark was being prepared, in which a few, that is, eight persons, were brought safely through water" (1 Pet. 3:20). Before God sent judgment, He waited about 75 years for the people at the time to willingly receive the free salvation that God had to offer through the ark. In the end, only eight people did so. God waited a long time before expressing anger.

Patience is an attribute of God. In contrast, patience is not natural to mankind. We are by nature impatient beings. We have short fuses and become angry very quickly. Once a person receives Christ as Savior and becomes a child of God (John 1:12), the Holy Spirit begins to live inside the person (2 Cor. 1:22). The book of Galatians describes the fruit of the Spirit: "But the fruit of the Spirit is love, joy, peace, patience, kindness, goodness, faithfulness, gentleness, self-control…" (Gal. 5:22-23). As we yield to the control of the Holy Spirit, we begin to exhibit the characteristics of God and begin seeing patience in ourselves. This is a work of God.

We need patience in our relationships, at home, at work, at school, and at church. We need to wait a long time before expressing anger. Our relationships do better when we leave anger out of them. That is why, many times in the New Testament, we are commanded to be patient with others: "…walk in a manner worthy of the calling to which you have been called, with all humility and gentleness, with patience, bearing with one another in love" (Eph. 4:1-2). Many other passages carry a similar instruction: 2 Cor. 6:6; Col. 1:11 and 3:12; Heb. 6:12; 1 Thess. 5:14; James 5:7. We even need patience to witness to the world about Christ. As we grow in the Lord, we will display more of His patience: "…that in me… Jesus Christ might display his perfect patience as an example to those who were to believe in him for eternal life" (1 Tim. 1:16). As the troubles of the world increase, we need patience to serve God while we await the return of the Lord. "You also, be patient. Establish your hearts, for the coming of the Lord is at hand" (James 5:8).

Jesus told a story where this word for patience plays a central role. Peter approached Jesus and asked him if it was acceptable to forgive his brother who has sinned against him seven times. Jesus answered to him, "I do not say to you seven times, but seventy-seven times" (Matt. 18:22). Jesus went on to tell a story about a king who was approached by a servant that owed him an enormous debt. On his knees, the servant begged the king, "Have patience with me, and I will pay you everything" (v. 26). In other words, the servant said: Wait a long time before expressing your anger, and I will pay you back. The king had compassion on the servant and forgave his debt. That servant walked free and encountered a fellow servant who owed him a small amount. The freed servant chose to demand to be paid back. The servant in debt replied, "Have patience with me, and I will pay you" (v. 29). In other words: Wait a long time before expressing anger, and I will pay you back. The freed servant decided he did not want to wait or be patient, and so in anger he put the debtor in prison until the debt would be paid.

When the king heard of this turn of events, he called the freed servant back and told him, "'You wicked servant! I forgave you all that debt because you pleaded with me. And should not you have had mercy on your fellow servant, as I had mercy on you?' And in anger his master delivered him to the jailers, until he should pay all his debt" (vv. 32-34). Patience is like a two-sided coin: The other side of patience is mercy. Patience and mercy are always together. When Jesus was done telling this story, he said to His disciples, "So also my heavenly Father will do to every one of you, if you do not forgive your brother from your heart" (v. 35).

God is a patient God. He waits a long time before expressing righteous anger. We are the recipients of that patience. God expects us to give to others what we receive from Him. When we are not patient with others, God is not pleased and there are negative consequences in our lives. We should not avoid patience. We should embrace it. We should be eager to grow in it. Patience is a remarkable characteristic of God. Without it, humankind would be lost in immediate judgment. Patience makes our relationships better. Patience is key in ministry. Let's eagerly ask God for more patience and for the ability to wait a long time before expressing anger. That is true patience. What relationship in your life needs to receive more patience from you? Is there a person in your life for whom you need to wait a long time before expressing anger?

Patience: Remaining Under the Life Challenges That God Allows

The late adventurer and author Tim Hansel, who lived with chronic pain for more than three decades, said, "Most of the Psalms were born in difficulty. Most of the Epistles were written in prisons. Most of the greatest thoughts of the greatest thinkers of all time had to pass through the fire. Bunyan wrote *Pilgrim's Progress* from jail. Florence Nightingale, too ill to move from her bed, reorganized the hospitals of England. Semi-paralyzed and under the constant menace of apoplexy, Pasteur was tireless in his attack on disease. Sometimes it seems that when God is about to make preeminent use of a person, he puts that person through the fire."[24]

These stories from these amazing people point to a second aspect of patience. The second Greek word in the New Testament translated several times into the word patience is the word *hypomone*, from the Greek roots *hypo* (under) and *meno* (remain, endure). This other meaning of the word patience is to remain under—to remain under what? To remain under the life challenges that God allows. Let's consider several passages referring to patience, each of which have the word *hypomone* in the Greek.

Perhaps you did not know this, but many overseas missionaries from many missionary agencies end their careers by the end of their first term. So many times, the reason they give up their calling, their training, and their investment of time and money is because they want to get away from their difficult coworkers; they can't get along with them. We are in great need of patience, the kind of patience that leads a person to endure. So many times, God's victory is just around the corner, but we are not there to see it because we left. We were defeated by our mental battles. We miss the blessing of spiritual growth, of seeing God turn something bad into something good, and of seeing God's abundant grace of forgiveness and healing. We miss it because we quit. We had no patience. You see this happen also in churches. There are individuals and families who will jump from church to church anytime a problem arises. They have no patient endurance. They are not willing to remain under the life challenges that God allows. God desires to do a work in their lives, but they don't want to be around to see God work, so they move on. The safest time to leave a ministry is when there are no problems—there is peace, and so we leave with peace and leave peace behind us. "For God is not a God of confusion but of peace..." (1 Cor. 14:33).

While I must say that sometimes it is the right thing to leave a harmful situation or a destructive relationship, so many people give up too easily. They give up on their relationships, their vocation, their loved ones, their calling, or their ministry just because circumstances became too difficult. When life becomes difficult, we should not run away. Instead, we should run to God. He is the one who is going to give us patience, the God-given ability to remain under the life challenges that God allows. God will give us His grace to endure. "Let us then with confidence draw near to the throne of grace, that we may receive mercy and find grace to help in time of need" (Heb. 4:16).

God desires for us to have patience. Paul says that when we patiently endure sufferings, we will experience the comfort of God, and others will also have His comfort. "If we are afflicted, it is for your comfort and salvation; and if we are comforted, it is for your comfort, which you experience when you patiently endure the same sufferings that we suffer" (2 Cor. 1:6).

God is doing a special work in our lives. God's goal is not for us to live a comfortable life on this earth for 70, 80, or 90 years and then go on to heaven. God's desire is to make us like Christ (2 Cor. 3:18). If a man wants to take a tree trunk and make a column for his house, he is going to cut, shave, carve, and sand it. Those rough actions result in a beautiful column with a noble purpose to support the house. God is cutting, carving, and sanding our lives to remove undesirable characteristics and to make us like Christ to be used for His divine purposes. That process can be painful at times and is going to include some suffering. God often sends people into our lives to be the sandpaper. Can you think of someone in your life that God has used as sandpaper? God wants us to remain under the life challenges that He allows. Over the ages, Christians have endured hardships for the glory of God. It's believed that at the First Council of Nicaea, an important church meeting in the fourth century A.D., of the 318 delegates who attended, fewer than a dozen had not lost an eye or a hand or did not limp on a leg lamed by torture for their Christian faith. "For it has been granted to you that for the sake of Christ you should not only believe in him but also suffer for his sake" (Phil. 1:29).

The Lord Jesus Himself had this kind of patience, "…the patient endurance… in Jesus" (Rev. 1:9). When Jesus was teaching His disciples, He told them about a group of people who, "…hearing the word, hold it fast in an honest and good heart, and bear fruit with patience" (Luke 8:15). There is no bearing fruit without patience. Ask any farmer. Farmers are trained in the skill of patience. They wait for the ground to be dry enough to plow, they wait for the right weather to plant, then they wait for the good Lord to send the rain and the sunshine. They must persevere through storms, floods, and droughts. They wait for the crop to be ripe and the weather to be just right to harvest. They are eventually rewarded for their patience with a good crop. There's no difference in our spiritual lives. When we remain under the life challenges that God allows, we are going to see God bring about spiritual fruit that can only be produced in the greenhouse of trials.

One of my favorite books in the Bible is the book of Acts. I love to see how the apostles and early disciples went about serving God filled with the Holy Spirit. Paul, an apostle, wrote, "The signs of a true apostle were performed among you with utmost patience…" (2 Cor. 12:12). The great ministry done by the apostles was performed with great patience while they remained under the life challenges that God allowed. In 2 Cor. 11:24-27, Paul presents a long list of painful experiences he went through while serving God. However, he also stated that even with the suffering he experienced, nothing "…will be able to separate us from the love of God in Christ Jesus our Lord" (Rom. 8:39). Paul invited Timothy and, ultimately, you and I to follow his example of patience: "You, however, have followed my teaching, my conduct, my aim in life, my faith, my patience…" (2 Tim. 3:10). Three times Paul asked God to remove his thorn in the flesh. The Lord responded, "My grace is sufficient for you, for my power is made perfect in weakness" (2 Cor. 12:9). Paul needed patience, and God gave it to him by His grace.

Perhaps you are ready to quit your ministry; you are too tired of the trials. You need to remember your calling and endure. Christian pastor and author Warren Wiersbe mentioned that nineteeth-century English evangelist Charles Spurgeon had a plaque on his bedroom wall with Isaiah 48:10 written on it: "I have chosen thee in the furnace of affliction." Wiersbe went on to say, "It is no mean thing to be chosen of God. God's choice makes chosen men choice men.... We are chosen, not in the palace, but in the furnace. In the furnace, beauty is marred, fashion is destroyed, strength is melted, glory is consumed; yet here eternal love reveals its secrets, and declares its choice."[25] God has chosen you to serve Him; you need to choose to remain. In the book of Revelation, the Lord Jesus had messages for several churches. To three of the churches, the Lord praised their patience (Rev. 2:2, 3, 19; 3:10). Here's an example: "I know you are enduring patiently and bearing up for my name's sake, and you have not grown weary" (Rev. 2:3). The Lord congratulated three churches because they remained under the life challenges that God allowed. They weren't perfect, but through the challenges they remained faithful and had patient endurance. One day in heaven the hardships will be exchanged for glory. "I consider that our present sufferings are not worth comparing with the glory that will be revealed in us.... But if we hope for what we do not yet have, we wait for it patiently" (Rom. 8:18, 25). We must wait for that glory with patience. We must remain under the life challenges that God allows.

Don't you want the Lord to say the same of you? That we lived this life with patient endurance? That we didn't run when things got tough, but remained under the life challenges that God allowed? I am not diminishing the trials you may be experiencing. I have had my share of them, and they are not easy. I have wanted to quit many times. I am reminding both of us that we have a Savior who has suffered patiently, too. He has given us the Holy Spirit and gives us His grace each day to enable us to obey God's instruction in Romans 12:12: "Rejoice in hope, be patient in tribulation, be constant in prayer." Will you remain under the challenges that God is allowing in your life?

God's Purposes in Seasons of Waiting

Years ago, I was at a United States airport and started chatting with a copilot (I don't remember the airline). I asked him about his training and career. I asked him if he was able to fly the airplane all by himself. He said yes. Then I asked him how many years he would have to serve as a copilot before he could become a pilot. He said that in the airline where he worked, he would have to serve as copilot for 11 years until he would be promoted to captain. That is eleven years of waiting!

Waiting must be one of the hardest things people have to do. Many mental battles are fought in seasons of waiting. I would even say that seasons of waiting can be a greenhouse where mental battles develop. The great New England preacher Phillips Brooks was noted for his poise and quiet manner. At times, however, even he suffered moments of frustration and irritability. One day a friend saw him feverishly pacing the floor like a caged lion. "What's the trouble, Mr. Brooks?" the friend asked. Brooks responded, "The trouble is that I'm in a hurry, but God isn't!"[26]

It seems that at times God allows seasons of waiting in our lives. The Bible reveals that great men and women of God went through seasons of waiting. Abraham waited 25 years for the promise of a son to be fulfilled. Joseph waited 13 years in prison for something he did not do. Moses waited 40 years in the desert before God sent him to Egypt to deliver the Hebrews from slavery. Moses, Caleb, and Joshua waited for the Promised Land for 40 years while wandering in the desert. David waited 15 years between the time he was anointed king and when he ascended to the throne of Israel. Jesus waited 30 years to begin his public ministry. Paul waited three years in Arabia before going to Jerusalem. Some of the greatest missionaries of history devotedly spread the seed of God's Word—and yet had to wait long periods before seeing the fruit of their efforts.

There is no doubt that those who walk with God go through seasons of waiting on God. Perhaps you feel that happened to you in 2020 when COVID-19 appeared and you found yourself in lockdown. Or perhaps you feel that you were already in a season of waiting even before the pandemic started. Perhaps you have been waiting for God to open doors of opportunity. Maybe you are waiting on God's leading for ministry.

I received a call from God to serve Him in ministry when I was 17. It was at a Youth for Christ leadership conference in Portugal organized by its director, my friend Moisés Gomes. Shortly after that, I went to Portuguese Bible Institute to prepare for ministry. Maryjane and I were married in 1985, and I thought for certain that we would get started in full-time ministry right away. God closed that door for nine years. I spent those nine years working as a businessman in Portugal, doing ministry on the side, waiting for God to open the door. Finally, nine years later, God began to stir our hearts, and after a season of prayer, we realized God was saying, "Now is the time." Through much prayer and a series of events, we were connected with the Christian organization in which I have now served for nearly three decades. In my story, there was divine purpose in our waiting. God was working in us and teaching us during those nine years. What should Christians do when they find themselves in a season of waiting? Let's take some lessons from Joseph's waiting season.

The Lord is with you as you wait; don't lose sight of that. As soon as Joseph was put in prison, the Bible states that "the Lord was with Joseph and showed him steadfast love…" (Gen. 39:21). Sometimes in seasons of waiting it feels like you are alone or abandoned. Don't trust your feelings. Trust God's Word when it says, "I will never leave you nor forsake you" (Heb. 13:5). The Lord was with Joseph as he waited in prison, and the Lord is with you as you wait on Him. He is "…Christ in you, the hope of glory" (Col. 1:27).

As you wait on the Lord, don't be inactive. There is work to do. Find out what God wants you to do while you are in a season of waiting. While in prison, Joseph took on a leadership role: "And the keeper of the prison put Joseph in charge of all the prisoners who were in the prison. Whatever was done there, he was the one who did it" (Gen. 39:22). In 2020 in many countries, the pandemic lockdown kept people from being able to get out of their houses. Nevertheless, isolation does not mean inactivity. I heard of stories from around the world of people reaching out to others using phone calls, video conferencing, and messaging apps. I know of a family in the Philippines that held Sunday services in their yard during the global lockdown with a microphone and speakers to minister to their neighbors. I received a report from Africa that group Bible clubs had stopped due to the pandemic, but that one individual had gone alone door-to-door to give Bible lessons for the children and to pick them up a few days later and drop off new ones. Many times, he was invited to speak to those families about Christ. Pastors became involved doing door-to-door work, too, when they could not have services for several months. Some report much time spent in the Word and in prayer for others. Joseph stayed busy in prison as he waited on God. As you wait on God to know what to do next, you need to stay busy helping others to the best of your ability. What does not make sense now may make sense in the future; we need to trust the sovereign God. British evangelist and author G. Campbell Morgan said, "Waiting for God is not laziness. Waiting for God is not going to sleep. Waiting for God is not the abandonment of effort. Waiting for God means, first, activity under command; second, readiness for any new command that may come…."[27]

Later in Joseph's story, he told his brothers, "… you meant evil against me, but God meant it for good, to bring it about that many people should be kept alive, as they are today" (Gen. 50:20). When you are waiting, you have few or no answers. Be assured of the fact that in the future you will be able to look back and see the hand of God in the waiting season and comprehend how God unfolds His purposes in your life. For now, while things don't yet make sense, trust the sovereign control of God and wait on Him. Bible scholar and author Wayne Stiles said, "Because the results of God's sovereignty are delayed, waiting remains an act of faith. We believe results will occur one day. By waiting on God, we affirm our belief in his providence. We trust his timetable. We hope in heaven. Waiting on God is inseparably bound to our belief in the sovereignty of God to bring about the good He promises."[28]

We need God's Word each day, but especially in seasons of waiting. The psalmist wrote, "I wait for the Lord, my soul waits, and in his word I hope" (Ps. 130:5). We want to hear from God as we wait. The truth of God's Word gives us hope, faith, confidence, and optimism about tomorrow. Here are a few of the many Bible verses on this topic:

- God will answer you: "…for you, O Lord, do I wait; it is you, O Lord my God, who will answer" (Ps. 38:15).
- God will deliver you: "Do not say, 'I will repay evil'; wait for the Lord, and he will deliver you" (Prov. 20:22).
- God will give you strength: "…they who wait for the Lord shall renew their strength; they shall mount up with wings like eagles; they shall run and not be weary; they shall walk and not faint" (Isa. 40:31).

We so often want immediate guidance so that we can make a decision, but instead we must wait for guidance to come. The reason you might not have everything you need to make a decision could be because today is not the day to make that decision. When the day to make the decision comes, God will lift the fog of uncertainty and allow you to see with clarity. Then you will be ready to make that decision. Lack of clarity is tied to timing. Maybe you are waiting at work for your idea to take off. Maybe other leaders fail to see the benefits you see. Such situations can be frustrating, and they can cause mental battles as you see other people's ideas move forward while yours remains in a waiting pattern. Seasons of waiting can cause much agitation on your mind.

As you wait on the Lord for His direction for the next step, remember that all Christians around the world have waiting hearts. All Christians are waiting for the return of their Savior, "waiting for our blessed hope, the appearing of the glory of our great God and Savior Jesus Christ" (Titus 2:13). We await with great expectation the return of the Lord Jesus, our salvation, "so Christ, having been offered once to bear the sins of many, will appear a second time, not to deal with sin but to save those who are eagerly waiting for him" (Heb. 9:28). Somehow this idea of collective waiting can help us in our individual seasons of waiting.

What should be our attitude as we wait on the Lord? One of sadness, worry, or despair? No! We can wait on God with joy. Rejoice while you wait, and rejoice when the Lord answers prayer and reveals His purposes. "It will be said on that day, 'Behold, this is our God; we have waited for him, that he might save us. This is the Lord; we have waited for him; let us be glad and rejoice in his salvation'" (Isa. 25:9). Campus pastor Ben Patterson said, "As we wait, it is critical that we keep our sense of humor in the fullest meaning of that word. When laughter goes, so does hope. When God reaffirms his promise to Abraham and Sarah, he restores not only their faith, but their ability to laugh as well. One goes with the other. Only the laughers can believe. Only the believers can laugh. The only thing worse than waiting is waiting without laughing."[29] Wait on the Lord with hope and with joy. He is faithful. He will come through at the right time.

God is at work in our seasons of waiting, growing faith in us. In Luke 18 Jesus told a parable to his disciples. The first thing he said was the purpose of this story: "And he told them a parable to the effect that they ought always to pray and not lose heart" (Luke 18:1). A woman wanted a judge to hear her case. The judge didn't want to hear it. The woman persisted until the judge gave in and helped her. The Lord concluded with these words: "Hear what the unrighteous judge says. And will not God give justice to his elect, who cry to him day and night? Will he delay long over them? I tell you, he will give justice to them speedily. Nevertheless, when the Son of Man comes, will he find faith on earth?" (Luke 18:6-8).

Remember, in this story Jesus is teaching the disciples about praying in seasons of waiting and not losing heart. Jesus is saying: Persevere, hang in there, and God will answer "speedily." Jesus ends with this somber statement: "Nevertheless, when the Son of Man comes, will he find faith on earth?" (Luke 18:8). What He is saying here is that faith grows in the seasons of waiting as we pray and trust God to show up at the right time. Faith and waiting on God are interlinked. May your mental battles and your troubles decrease and your faith grow as you wait on the Lord. How are you actively trusting God in your season of waiting?

Renewing the Mind

The human body is exposed to toxic substances in the environment, and the body also produces toxins through its various chemical reactions. For our bodies to survive, they must eliminate those toxins. This process is called "detoxification" and is accomplished by the key organs of the kidneys, skin, colon, lungs, and liver. Our God created our bodies in a brilliant way with a built-in self-purification system.

What about our minds? Have you ever thought of what God planned for detoxing our minds? Just like our bodies, our minds need detoxification. Our minds are bombarded every day with information. Some information is good, and some is bad. As Christians, we have three enemies—the world, Satan, and the flesh. Our mind gets toxic deposits from those three sources on a regular basis. These deposits fuel mental battles like dry wood fuels a fire.

The Bible teaches that the world system is anti-Christ and anti-Christian. Jesus told His disciples, "If you were of the world, the world would love you as its own; but because you are not of the world, but I chose you out of the world, therefore the world hates you" (John 15:19). Satan throws flaming darts at Christians (Eph. 6:16); these are wrong thoughts or temptations. In Acts 5 we read an example of this: "But Peter said, 'Ananias, why has Satan filled your heart to lie to the Holy Spirit…?" (Acts 5:3). Our flesh and its desires can be a source of wrong thinking that leads to wrong decisions. "For the desires of the flesh are against the Spirit, and the desires of the Spirit are against the flesh, for these are opposed to each other, to keep you from doing the things you want to do" (Gal. 5:17).

The anti-Christian messages of the world, the wrong thoughts from Satan, and the desires of the flesh leave many toxins in our minds and hearts. Most of those toxins are lies; they are untruths. Daily we must remove those toxins from our minds and hearts, or the result will be rampant wrong thinking. Wrong thinking leads to negative emotions, and negative emotions propel us to wrong decisions. Wrong decisions quickly decay our quality of life, and they are not pleasing to the Lord.

God knows that our minds and hearts need daily removal of toxins. The Lord wants us to "not be conformed to this world, but be transformed by the renewal of your mind…" (Rom. 12:2). How do we renew our minds? How do we take out the bad and put in the good? The Lord Jesus said that it is God's Word that does the work of washing and cleansing. "Christ loved the church and gave himself up for her to make her holy, cleansing her by the washing with water through the word" (Eph. 5:25-26). It is when we read God's Word each day that the Spirit of God begins to use the truth of the Bible to point out mental toxins and to remove and replace them with the truth of God's Word.

The problem is that many people think they have no mental toxins. That is part of the deception. Your mind can be filled with wrong thinking, and you believe your thinking is fine. You need an outside power—a transcendent, cleansing power—to point out the toxins and remove them. Nothing can do that divine work but the Bible. "For the word of God is alive and powerful. It is sharper than the sharpest two-edged sword, cutting between soul and spirit, between joint and marrow. It exposes our innermost thoughts and desires" (Heb. 4:12).

Satan, the world, and the flesh will do everything they can to keep you away from the daily reading of God's Word. You will talk yourself into a thousand reasons why you do not need to read the Bible. Perhaps you find reasons such as: "I am too busy"; "I will listen to it Sunday morning at church"; "Social media is a lot more exciting"; "I will start tomorrow"; or "I don't need to read it because I know it." Knowing is the beginning, not the destination. One of the reasons we read the Word every day is for cleansing purposes. The Lord said, "Already you are clean because of the word that I have spoken to you" (John 15:3). The Word cleanses. We read it every day so that our mind can be renewed: "…to be renewed in the spirit of your minds" (Eph. 4:23). We read it because ultimate success comes when we obey it: "Having purified your souls by your obedience to the truth…" (1 Pet. 1:22). In my late teens, a friend wrote in my Bible, "This book will keep you from sin, or sin will keep you from this book." After living five decades as a Christian, observing my heart, and watching many other lives, I agree with that statement. We need to be in the Word of God each day for our minds to be cleansed. "How can a young man keep his way pure? By guarding it according to your word" (Ps. 119:9).

The goal of the Christian life is not Bible knowledge. The goal for us as disciples of Christ is obedience to God. Reading the Bible is a means to the goal of obedience. Jesus Himself said about His disciples, "…teaching them to observe all that I have commanded you" (Matt. 28:20). The most beautiful sermon ever preached is the Sermon on the Mount, and the preacher was the Lord Jesus Christ Himself. This amazing sermon is found in Matthew 5-7. What would be the perfect conclusion for this divine sermon? The Lord chose a story.

"Everyone then who hears these words of mine and does them will be like a wise man who built his house on the rock. And the rain fell, and the floods came, and the winds blew and beat on that house, but it did not fall, because it had been founded on the rock. And everyone who hears these words of mine and does not do them will be like a foolish man who built his house on the sand. And the rain fell, and the floods came, and the winds blew and beat against that house, and it fell, and great was the fall of it" (Matt. 7:24-27).

In this story Jesus said that there are two types of people in the audience, the one "who hears these words of mine and does them" and the one "who hears these words of mine and does not do them." He went on to explain that obedience is the key for success. You obey the words of Christ, and your life is good and strong. You disobey the words of Christ, and your life will fall apart. Jesus was saying that knowing the Bible is insufficient. The ultimate goal is not to *know* the Bible; it is to *obey* the Bible. We read the Bible and study the Bible so our minds can be renewed and so that we will obey the Bible and please God.

A full-time ministry staff person shared this true story with me about how our minds as Christians can get so off into wrong thinking, and it is the Word of God that can correct our thinking and put us on the right path.

In my first couple years of ministry, I was super excited to serve. But I was also fighting serious depression. I had such great respect for the ministry and held myself to such a high standard that I was constantly focused on how I had failed. Whether it was too long of a Bible lesson for the teacher training demonstration or whether I was running late, not getting all my applications in a Bible lesson, or saying the wrong thing to one of the volunteers, I remembered every detail and would beat myself up for each thing for weeks on end. In addition to many lonely hours living by myself, struggling to take care of myself, this turned into a deep, dark depression. Though I often contemplated running away from life or even ending life, I still very vividly remember the morning that I came inches from purposely making my death look like an accident. I had it all planned. I didn't leave a note, so it wouldn't even look like a suicide, but so I could end it all. Driving down the road, I knew a particular corner of this weekly route that had a sharp turn. Missing that turn would mean slamming into the side of a rocky cliff, and unbuckling and leaning out of the way of the airbags would mean I would avoid any lifesaving features of my car. I still remember the moment of decision as I neared that curve: All I had to do was not turn the steering wheel. At the last possible moment, I made the corner, but wept knowing how close I had come to death. I went on with the ministry journey that morning and taught the teacher training class, but my next stop was to meet with one of my pastors for some emergency counseling.

After providing me with some simple tools to combat the depression, the first passage he gave me to study was 2 Peter 1:3, that God has given me everything I need for life and godliness. As he explained, no matter what I felt about my skills or abilities, I had been given from God everything I would ever need to live a life pleasing to Him. At first, I was in such a hole that I couldn't even comprehend how this truth would even apply to my life. Over the next several weeks of counseling,

> *though, I was taught to combat every lie I was believing about my skills and abilities with the truth of God's Word. It couldn't be a one-and-done moment of decision and then I was magically cured. Multiple times a day, I had to recognize that I was believing a lie about myself when I started to put myself down and get mad at myself for messing up yet again. In each of those moments, I had to start reminding myself of the truth of God's Word, gradually replacing the lies with His truth. Later, I would learn to call this "taking every thought captive" (2 Cor. 10:5). Of course, I've struggled in other areas, too, but the principle of renewing my mind with the truth of God's Word that I learned in that dark tunnel was so vivid that it has helped me walk through those other struggles as well.* [30]

I should make a comment concerning depression. A good number of people involved in different aspects of ministry suffer from different levels of depression. There is a medical aspect to it, and the individual should seek medical help. For all of us, the mental battles are true, and they are real. Just like our bodies, our minds need detoxification. God did not give us a special organ in our bodies for that purpose; He gave us the Word of God. The habit of reading and studying God's Word every day has the divine purpose of renewing our minds.

People in ministry need to be careful when they only pick up the Bible to prepare a message or a devotional to share with a group. It is important for people in ministry to pick up the Bible for the sole purpose of allowing God to speak to their hearts. We are all weary of hearing stories of ministry leaders whose personal lives, marriages, and ministries were lost because of poor decisions they made. While wrong thinking was increasing in their minds and deception was building in their hearts, they were ministering God's Word to other people. Somehow, they were not allowing the Word of God to cleanse their own minds. In the words of Solomon, "they made me keeper of the vineyards, but my own vineyard I have not kept!" (Songs 1:6). Make sure your time in the Word is not rushed and mechanical. Allow the Spirit of God to minister to your soul as you spend time in His Word. How has the Spirit of God been speaking to you through God's Word in your time spent in the Bible?

The Need for Strength and Courage

The Prussian king Frederick the Great was widely known as an agnostic. By contrast, General Von Zealand, one of his most trusted officers, was a devout Christian. Thus it was that during a festive gathering the king began making crude jokes about Christ until everyone was rocking with laughter—all but Von Zealand, that is. Finally, he arose and addressed the king: "Sire, you know I have not feared death. I have fought and won 38 battles for you. I am an old man; I shall soon have to go into the presence of One greater than you, the mighty God who saved me from my sin, the Lord Jesus Christ whom you are blaspheming. I salute you, sire, as an old man who loves his Savior, on the edge of eternity." The place went silent, and with a trembling voice the king replied, "General Von Zealand—I beg your pardon! I beg your pardon!" And with that the party quietly ended.[31] Risking his own position before the king, this Christian general spoke up with courage and strength seeking to honor the King of kings. I love this moment of strength and courage of a godly leader.

Some mental battles take place because we feel we lack the strength and courage to serve or to lead. Maybe the people we are supposed to lead lack confidence in our ability to lead. Maybe we struggle with fear, or we are insecure in our leadership. We lack confidence and strength. This happens many times even in people who appear outwardly confident.

After the death of Moses, God chose Joshua to be the new leader of Israel. Joshua knew the task was not going to be easy, and he was obviously struggling with fear, perhaps even feeling inadequate. Leading the people of Israel was going to be challenging. How many of us would like to follow in the footsteps of the man who received the Ten Commandments from God? The Lord began by giving a message to Joshua. We read about that in the first verses of the book of Joshua. In this rich message God told Joshua, not once, not twice, but three times to be strong and courageous. Twice also in that message God emphasized to Joshua that He would be with him. The Lord's presence would be a constant. There are other vital truths in God's communication to Joshua, but those two points seem to be of special importance that warranted repetition by God.

Joshua's fear was understandable. He had a big and challenging task in front of him. Perhaps you feel the same way as a leader. So many things to accomplish, so many people problems, so many difficult tasks, so few resources, and so much opposition. Perhaps there are days that you want to curl up and spend the day in bed. We have all been there. Let's consider God's message to Joshua in Joshua 1:5-9:

No man shall be able to stand before you all the days of your life. Just as I was with Moses, so I will be with you. I will not leave you or forsake you. Be strong and courageous, for you shall cause this people to inherit the land that I swore to their fathers to give them. Only be strong and very courageous, being careful to do according to all the law that Moses my servant commanded you. Do not turn from it to the right hand or to the left, that you may have good success wherever you go. This Book of the Law shall not depart from your mouth, but you shall meditate on it day and night, so that you may be careful to do according to all that is written in it. For then you will make your way prosperous, and then you will have good success. Have I not commanded you? Be strong and courageous. Do not be frightened, and do not be dismayed, for the Lord your God is with you wherever you go.

Twice God told Joshua that the Lord would be with him. It was of extreme importance that Joshua would remember that. Joshua was not alone. The presence of God would give him strength for the challenges ahead. He was going to be doing God's work, and God was going to be with him. The presence of God would also be the fuel for Joshua to obey the Lord's instruction to be strong and courageous. Three times God told Joshua to be strong and courageous. He needed that attitude to lead with confidence and to be followed by God's people.

In my ministry leadership assignments, I have been in seasons of courage and strength and seasons of fear and weakness. I remember one time I was facing some difficult challenges, and I went into a prayer room alone with the Bible open to Joshua 1, telling myself out loud several times, "Moisés, you need to be strong and courageous! The Lord is with you." Attitude is important in leadership. We know we are weak and frail, but we can be filled with the strength and courage that comes from the Lord. We must get up and move forward by faith, doing what we need to do, knowing that when we get to those scary moments, God is going to provide all we need, including strength and courage. Strength and courage come when we are focused on the fact that

God is with us, He is strong, and He gives us His strength. Here are a few passages that remind us that God is our source of strength:

- "Finally, be strong in the Lord and in the strength of his might" (Eph. 6:10).
- "I can do all things through him who strengthens me" (Phil. 4:13).
- "I thank him who has given me strength, Christ Jesus our Lord, because he judged me faithful, appointing me to his service" (1 Tim. 1:12).

We must remember that leadership is not about us. We are simple tools in the hands of a mighty God with eternal purposes that will be accomplished no matter what. He doesn't need us, but He loves to use weak vessels so that, in the end, He gets the glory and we get His blessing.

After receiving his leadership commission from God, Joshua told the officers of the people to begin preparations, for they would soon be departing. Then he told the leaders of the two and a half tribes that were settled east of the Jordan that the men of those tribes needed to also cross the Jordan and help the other tribes conquer their land. After the new leader of the nation of Israel had given his first instructions to the leaders and the people, we read about their response to Joshua. Would they be willing to follow Joshua's leadership? Would they rebel? Would they present Joshua with conditions? They answered Joshua that they would obey him and follow his leadership, but they told Joshua that they had two conditions before they would accept Joshua as their leader: "Only may the Lord your God be with you, as he was with Moses" (Josh. 1:17) and "Only be strong and courageous" (Josh. 1:18). Amazing! The two messages God gave Joshua repeatedly were exactly the same two requests the Israelites needed most from Joshua, their new leader.

God knows what you need, and God knows what the people you are going to lead need. We know the rest of the story. Joshua led the people in a godly way, and God gave him success. We, too, need to walk with God faithfully and lead with strength and courage. Our hearts and minds need to replace fear with courage. Our strength and courage do not come from our degrees, ministry experience, or past accomplishments. Divine strength and courage come from your walk in the presence of Almighty God. God asks for strength and courage from you, and your team needs it, too. For example, when you and your team face a major challenge, don't show panic and fear; instead, give them assuring words: "The Lord is with us, and He is going to help us through this challenge." Your words and attitude can cause the team to be confident in the Lord. What will you do to draw strength and courage from the presence of the Lord?

Ideas of God Versus Ideas of Men

When a homeowner wants to expand his living space, he will hire a company to come do the work. Suppose he wants to bring down some walls and create a more open living space. He will have to check if any of those walls are load-bearing walls. If they are not load-bearing walls, they can easily be taken down so the space can be redesigned. But if one of those walls is a load-bearing wall, it must be left alone. Otherwise, taking down that wall could take down the whole house. In this chapter I want to talk about some ideas that are like load-bearing walls. Whatever happens, they must keep standing.

The title of this chapter seems strange, doesn't it? How can the ideas of God be defeated by the ideas of men? It seems impossible. It is not the ideas themselves that can be defeated, but those principles can be ignored, disregarded, overlooked, or set aside in the hearts of ministry leaders set on implementing their own ideas. All leaders want to make changes. All leaders have unique ideas they would love to see implemented. Those ideas need to be examined in light of the Scriptures and in the scrutiny of a multitude of counselors. Much pain, stress, and heartbreak happen in the hearts of both leaders and those who are led when, in the eagerness to push men's ideas, God's ideas get trampled. This is a subtle, yet dangerous mental battle.

Most of us have witnessed or heard of a church split or a major confrontation among people in a ministry. We have seen the devastating impact of such conflicts in ministries and the lives of so many people. This happens when God's eternal ideas of love, forgiveness, and unity are trampled because the ideas of a leader or of someone else must be implemented at all costs.

What are those foundational ideas of God, those spiritual load-bearing walls that must always be upheld, no matter the changes leaders seek to implement? The relationships in the body of Christ are of great priority and must be guarded and nurtured. There are three powerful biblical truths that support all our relationships. They are the foundation for healthy relationships, which are so important in life. Everything we accomplish for God's Kingdom is done through relationships. These foundational ideas of God support our Christian life and are constantly under attack from three enemies: the world, the flesh, and the devil. We must hold on to these divine ideas very tightly. Let me present to you those three foundational ideas of God: unity, forgiveness, and love.

#1: Unity

The first idea of God is for Christians to build unity like the Holy Spirit does. In Samson's day, he tied the tales of foxes together to set fire to the fields of the Philistines. The foxes were together, but they had no unity, so they scattered in various directions. Sometimes we are together in our ministry team, but we lack unity, and that is not good. We must be devoted with all our hearts, minds, and strength to do whatever it takes to build and guard unity in the body of Christ. "With all humility and gentleness, with patience, bearing with one another in love, eager to maintain the unity of the Spirit in the bond of peace" (Eph. 4:2-3). Notice the words "eager to maintain unity." Are you eager to maintain unity? Are you being diligent and intentional about it? "Let us therefore make every effort to do what leads to peace and to mutual edification" (Rom. 14:19 NIV).

Pursuing unity in the body of Christ is serious business. It requires extreme commitment, and we need to make every effort to stay unified. This is what God thinks of unity: "Behold, how good and pleasant it is when brothers dwell in unity" (Ps. 133:1). In Jesus Christ's priestly prayer in John 17, He prayed for our unity four times. For example, "I in them and you in me, that they may become perfectly one, so that the world may know that you sent me and loved them even as you loved me" (John 17:23). Why should believers be devoted to unity? Because of the unity experienced by the Godhead, and so that the world will see Christ. We have to pursue with all our hearts that which is so dear to the heart of God: unity in the body of Christ.

When parents want to emphasize something important to their children, they will teach it from both the positive and the negative viewpoints. For example, "Timmy, when you cross the street, be sure to look both ways for traffic"—this is teaching from a positive perspective. "If you cross the street without looking both ways, you are not going to play with your friends for a week"—this is teaching from the negative side. Parents use both because they are trying to emphasize the importance of the principles they are teaching.

When God teaches a fundamental spiritual principle, He also teaches it from the positive side and from the negative side.

Following is the teaching on unity from the negative side. Proverbs 6:16-19 says, "There are six things that the Lord hates, seven that are an abomination to him." The seventh thing that is an abomination to Him is "one who sows discord among brothers" (v. 19). God thinks the person who builds unity is good and pleasant. God thinks of the person who sows discord as "an abomination." Here is more of God's negative teaching on unity: "I appeal to you, brothers, to watch out for those who cause divisions and create obstacles contrary to the doctrine that you have been taught; avoid them" (Rom. 16:17). God says to avoid those who cause divisions: "As for a person who stirs up division, after warning him once and then twice, have nothing more to do with him" (Titus 3:10). Have nothing to do with people who stir up division! This is a very serious matter. The Holy Spirit is building unity, and God wants you and I to join Him in that work in all our relationships. Spiritual unity is one of those foundational ideas of God that is more important than any wonderful new idea a leader may try to implement.

Theologian and reformer John Calvin, who saw that the devil's chief device was disunity and division and who preached that there should be friendly fellowship for all ministers of Christ, made a similar point in a letter to a trusted colleague: "Among Christians there ought to be so great a dislike of schism, as that they may always avoid it so fast as lies in their power…."[32]

#2: Forgiveness

The second idea of God, another spiritual load-bearing wall, is for Christians to forgive like Jesus forgives. People in general desire forgiveness. There's a Spanish story of a father and son who had become estranged. The son ran away, and the father set off to find him. He searched for months to no avail. Finally, in a last desperate effort to find him, the father put an ad in a Madrid newspaper. The ad read: "Dear Paco, meet me in front of this newspaper office at noon on Saturday. All is forgiven. I love you. Your Father." That Saturday, eight hundred Pacos showed up looking for forgiveness and love from their fathers.[33] People are hungry for forgiveness.

Christians are called to be forgiving. "Be kind to one another, tenderhearted, forgiving one another, as God in Christ forgave you" (Eph. 4:32). "Bearing with one another and, if one has a complaint against another, forgiving each other; as the Lord has forgiven you, so you also must forgive" (Col. 3:13). Notice that God's command for us to forgive our brothers and sisters is given *because* He first forgave us. Forgiveness is required, but it is not easy. Erwin W. Lutzer, pastor emeritus of Chicago's Moody Church, said, "Forgiveness is one of the most difficult assignments you will ever be given."[34] British writer, scholar, and theologian C.S. Lewis wrote these words: "Everyone says forgiveness is a lovely idea, until they have something to forgive...."[35]

Forgiving someone is hard, but it is part of who we are. It is in our DNA as Christians. It makes no sense when a Christian worker goes out to teach the Bible and, at the same time, does not forgive a Christian brother. The worker tells people about the power of the Gospel of reconciliation and that this Gospel can reconcile people with God and with other people, then goes back to the office and is unwilling to reconcile with a brother or sister. Do you know what God says about this? It's impossible! Let me show you where the Bible says that. With a parable, Jesus tried to explain the impossibility for a Christian to not be willing to forgive. This is the negative side of the teaching on forgiveness.

In Matthew 18:23-35, the Lord Jesus tells of a servant who owed a great debt and asked the king for mercy. The king forgave him his entire debt. That servant went out and did not forgive a much smaller debt someone owed him. The king heard about it and showed him his hypocrisy and lack of forgiveness. The wicked servant was sent to jail to pay his debt. "So also my heavenly Father will do to every one of you, if you do not forgive your brother from your heart" (Matt. 18:35).

After all my sin that God has forgiven me, when I am unwilling to forgive my brother or sister, I am the wicked servant. Let the words of our Savior sink in: "So also my heavenly Father will do to every one of you [Christians], if you do not forgive your brother from your heart" (Matt. 18:35). How many Christians experience pain, heartache, and turmoil because they don't want to forgive? If I don't forgive, I, too, can be thrown into prison, though most of the time the prison is one of resentment or bitterness because I am unwilling to forgive.

Jesus emphasized this same point at another time. Right after He taught his disciples how to pray, He added some additional teaching about one aspect of that prayer, the part about forgiveness: "For if you forgive others their trespasses, your heavenly Father will also forgive you, but if you do not forgive others their trespasses, neither will your Father forgive your trespasses" (Matt. 6:14-15). God is saying that it is impossible for a Christian not to forgive. If you don't forgive your brother, God won't forgive you. Forgiveness must be the hallmark of a Christian.

Christians ought to be known as people who forgive. Are you forgiving like you have been forgiven? Are you giving grace and mercy to others as God has given you grace and mercy? Who do you need to forgive? No ministry leader's idea should take precedence over God's idea of forgiveness.

#3: Love

The third idea of God is for Christians to love like God loves. When there are battles among people in a church or ministry, love becomes forgotten as people push for their ideas while forgetting God's idea of love. Can a Christian stop loving another Christian? Yes, I have seen it happen several times. These are the greatest commandments: "And you shall love the Lord your God with all your heart and with all your soul and with all your mind and with all your strength.' The second is this: 'You shall love your neighbor as yourself.' There is no other commandment greater than these" (Mark 12:30-31). Love is the greatest commandment, and no other is more important. Why? The Bible commands us to love others because God is love. "Beloved, let us love one another, for love is from God, and whoever loves has been born of God and knows God" (1 John 4:7). "A new commandment I give to you, that you love one another: just as I have loved you, you also are to love one another" (John 13:34). How do you love others? How do you love others when they are being difficult?

Here's the negative teaching about the importance of love: "We know that we have passed out of death into life, because we love the brothers. Whoever does not love abides in death. Everyone who hates his brother is a murderer, and you know that no murderer has eternal life abiding in him" (1 John 3:14-15). "Anyone who does not love does not know God, because God is love" (1 John 4:8). These are very strong texts concerning loving others, even in the midst of disagreements. You might be thinking: *This doesn't apply to me. I love everybody.* Let's look at the standard. Read the biblical text, putting your name in it. If your name is John, it would read like this: John is patient and kind; John does not envy or boast; John is not arrogant or rude. John does not insist on his own way; John is not irritable or resentful; John does not rejoice at wrongdoing; John rejoices with the truth. John bears all things, John believes all things, John hopes all things, John endures all things (based on 1 Cor. 13:4-7). Are you loving others this way, the same way Jesus loves you? True love is sacrificial.

Aristides de Sousa Mendes was one of the great heroes of World War II. As the Portuguese consul stationed in Bordeaux, France, he found himself confronted in May and June of 1940 with the reality of many thousands of refugees outside the Portuguese consulate attempting to escape the horrors of the Nazi military advance. These people were in desperate need of visas to get out of France, and a Portuguese visa would allow them safe passage through Spain to Lisbon, the capital of Portugal, where they could find liberty to travel to other parts of the globe.

> *Portugal, officially neutral, yet unofficially pro-Hitler and under the dictatorial rule of António de Oliveira Salazar, issued a directive—the infamous "Circular 14"—to all its diplomats to deny safe haven to refugees, explicitly stating that Jews, Russians, and stateless people could not freely return to their countries of origin. Aristides de Sousa Mendes' act of heroism was to defy these inhumane orders and follow his conscience instead. "I would rather stand with God against Man than with Man against God," he declared.*
>
> *In all, Sousa Mendes issued thousands of visas during that time, with the period of highest intensity lasting around the 12 days from June 12 to 23, 1940. This heroic feat was*

> *characterized by the Holocaust historian Yehuda Bauer as "perhaps the largest rescue action by a single individual during the Holocaust."*
>
> *For his act of defiance, Sousa Mendes was severely punished by Salazar, stripped of his diplomatic position, and forbidden from earning a living. He had 15 children who were themselves blacklisted and prevented from attending university or finding meaningful work. In this way, what was once an illustrious and well-respected family—one of the great families of Portugal—was crushed and destroyed. The family's ancestral home, known as "Casa do Passal," was repossessed by the bank and eventually sold to cover debts.*
>
> *Before his death in 1954, Sousa Mendes asked his children to clear his name and have the honor of the family restored. His sons and daughters, along with their children—now scattered all over the globe—have fought for decades to have his deeds posthumously recognized.*[36]

That is sacrificial love: sacrificing yourself to bless others. God loves us sacrificially; He gave His Son's life. Do you love like God loves? We must love our brothers, our sisters and those who are lost in a sacrificial way.

These three eternal spiritual principles are essential to the character of a Christian, woven into the fiber of our beings. We cannot stop seeking unity, forgiveness, and love. We cannot stop seeking to display the work of God, Jesus, and the Holy Spirit in what we do and say. Yet our three enemies—the world, the flesh, and the devil—will attack those truths in our minds day and night. Jesus is always pursuing unity, forgiveness, and love. Ministry leaders also need to pursue and guard these valuable principles with all their might.

At times ministry leaders are trying to push a ministry idea or make a change they think is going to transform or save the ministry. Perhaps they are experiencing a mental battle. Perhaps there is wrong thinking involved. They are not passing their ideas by the test of the multitude of counselors, and the people problems start happening. People are angry. People get pushed aside. People get hurt. Unity is gone, love is lost, and forgiveness is forgotten. All this occurs because someone is pushing their ideas above all else. When that happens, the ideas of men have trumped the ideas of God. This should never, ever happen. The opposite should happen: The ideas of God need to be upheld, and the ideas of men need to change to make sure the eternal ideas of God remain intact. The kind of ministry leader who values unity, forgiveness, and love will be blessed by God. Their ministry will be blessed by God. How are you safeguarding God's ideas of unity, forgiveness, and love above all others in your ministry?

Conflicts, Quarrels, and Fights

One day I traveled from my ministry's international headquarters to a U.S. state to help with a quarrel between a state team and a local area team. I met with the state team first. They felt they were in the right and even questioned why it was necessary for me to be there. In the afternoon I traveled to a home to meet with the local team. After a light lunch, it was time for the meeting to start, and a person put a very thick binder in front of me. I think it was the thickest binder I had ever seen, perhaps four inches thick. When the person placed it in front of me, he said, "It's all in here!" What that person meant was that all the documents that demonstrated that "we are right, and they are wrong" were in there. Many quarrels had gone on to fill such a thick binder.

Sometimes mental battles produce quarrels and fights, and sometimes quarrels and fights produce mental battles. We live in a time of many quarrels and fights. There are fights on social media, fights in neighborhoods, fights at school or at work, fights in families, fights in churches, and fights in Christian organizations. If you are involved in any kind of ministry, you will run into quarrels and fights. In Scripture, God speaks not only to why these fights happen, but also tells us what to do about these quarrels and fights. James wrote about this in James 4. He begins this chapter with a question: "What causes quarrels and what causes fights among you?" (James 4:1). James' question is about the root cause of the fights. Next, he describes three sources of the fights.

The first source of quarrels and fights is the flesh. In the first three verses, James uses the word "passions" to refer to our flesh: "Is it not this, that your passions are at war within you? You desire and do not have, so you murder. You covet and cannot obtain, so you fight and quarrel. You do not have, because you do not ask. You ask and do not receive, because you ask wrongly, to spend it on your passions" (James 4:1-3). James says that we are at war within ourselves: "your passions are at war within you." The war within ourselves triggers wars with others and can cause wars in the ministry. When I walk into a room to join my coworkers, I bring the potential for conflict within me.

One of my favorite illustrations on this topic is the man who was lost at sea and ended up on a deserted island for 10 years.

> *There was once a man who had been shipwrecked on an uninhabited desert island. There he lived alone for 10years before finally being rescued by a passing aircraft. Before leaving the island, one of the rescuers asked if they could see where the man had lived during his time on the island, and so he brought the small group to a clearing where there were three buildings.*
>
> *Pointing to the first, he said, "This was my home; I built it when I first moved here all those years ago."*
>
> *"What about the building beside it?" asked one of the rescuers.*
>
> *"Oh, that is where I would worship every week," he replied.*

> *"And the building beside that?"*
>
> *"Don't bring that up," replied the man in an agitated tone. "That is where I used to worship."*[37]

Conflict begins within ourselves, and it spreads to others.

The war within ourselves causes wars in the ministry. James goes on to say that the essence of sin is selfishness. Selfish desires lead to wrong actions. They even lead to wrong, selfish prayers. Selfish living and selfish prayer always lead to quarrels. If there is war on the inside, there will ultimately be war on the outside. Many church, organization, or family problems would be solved if people would only look into their own hearts and see the battles raging there. In the previous chapter, James wrote, "But, if you have bitter jealousy and selfish ambition in your hearts, do not boast and be false to the truth. This is not the wisdom that comes down from above, but is earthly, unspiritual, demonic. For where jealousy and selfish ambition exist, there will be disorder and every vile practice" (James 3:14-16).

The second source of quarrels and fights is the world. James goes on to write, "You adulterous people! Do you not know that friendship with the world is enmity with God? Therefore, whoever wishes to be a friend of the world makes himself an enemy of God. Or do you suppose it is to no purpose that the Scripture says, 'He yearns jealously over the spirit that he has made to dwell in us'? But he gives more grace. Therefore, it says, 'God opposes the proud but gives grace to the humble'" (James 4:4-6).

Twice in this text, James said that loving the world makes our relationship with God adversarial. There are several uses of the word "world." In these verses, "world" refers to human society apart from God. The world system tends to be anti-God; therefore, the world is the enemy of God.

While writing about James 4 in his commentary, Warren Wiersbe shares how a Christian gets involved with the world gradually, which can be seen throughout the New Testament. First, he begins with friendship with the world (James 4:4), then the believer becomes "stained" by the world (James 1:27) so that he can gain approval by the world. This leads to loving the world (1 John 2:15-17), and, ultimately, when we love the world, we conform to the world (Romans 12:2). Worldly thinking and worldly affections cause quarrels and fights among Christians. Here's good news: Christ can give us victory over the world, but we must be aware of the gradual lure of the world. Twentieth-century Presbyterian pastor Donald Grey Barnhouse said:

> *Some years ago, musicians noted that errand boys in a certain part of London all whistled out of tune as they went about their work. It was talked about, and someone suggested that it was because the bells of Westminster were slightly out of tune. Something had gone wrong with the chimes, and they were discordant. The boys did not know there was anything wrong with the peals, and quite unconsciously they had copied their pitch.*

So we tend to copy the people with whom we associate; we borrow thoughts from the books we read and the programs to which we listen, almost without knowing it. God has given us His Word which is the absolute pitch of life and living. If we learn to sing by it, we shall easily detect the false in all of the music of the world.[38]

The third source of quarrels and fights is the devil. James stated, "Submit yourselves therefore to God. Resist the devil, and he will flee from you" (James 4:7). Pride is Satan's great sin. He fell because of pride, and he seeks to cause Christians to fall because of pride. God wants us to be humble; Satan wants us to be proud. Many times, pride sneaks into ministry, and it can creep into the hearts of ministry leaders.

Warren Wiersbe said, "We have too many 'celebrities' and not enough servants—'nine-day wonders' that may flash across the scene for a time and then disappear. Before God works through us, he works in us, because the work that we do is the outgrowth of the life that we live."[39] We must guard our hearts from pride.

James 4 started with the question, "What causes quarrels and what causes fights among you?" In the following verses, he gives us the answer: the world, the devil, and the flesh! Christ has delivered us from them, but they still attack us. How can we overcome them? How can we be friends with God and enemies of the world, the flesh, and the devil? In this passage God gave us seven steps for us to take as part of the solution. Notice that these verbs are in the imperative form, so these actions are not optional. They are a mandate!

First, submit to God. "Submit yourselves therefore to God…" (James 4:7). If we are going to have victory over quarrels and fights, selfish ambition needs to be replaced with spiritual submission. Submission has become a bad word in today's culture. A few years back, we did a large evangelistic outreach in a major city on the West Coast. A group of atheists that opposed our work published an article in a magazine with many accusations against our Christian organization. I was surprised to read one of them: "They even teach the children to submit to authority." I thought submission to authority was a good thing. Don't we want elementary school children to obey their teachers? Don't we want drivers to obey the STOP traffic sign? Don't we want children to obey their parents? Don't we want soldiers to obey their leaders? The world, in opposition to God, is communicating that submission to authority is negative. Unfortunately, that teaching quickly seeps into the church. When we submit to God, we are in a humble position of power and authority. Submission to God also means submission to His Word.

Second, resist the devil. "Resist the devil, and he will flee from you" (James 4:7). If we are going to have victory over quarrels and fights, we must resist the devil. Because of the complexity of this command, we have an entire chapter dedicated to the topic, but suffice it to say this part of our responsibility is vital. In the coming chapter "Resist the Devil and He Will Flee From You," we will learn to follow the example of Christ in dealing with the enemy of our souls.

Third, draw near to God. "Draw near to God, and he will draw near to you" (James 4:8). If we are going to have victory over quarrels and fights, we need to draw near to God. In the middle of a fight, our attention is on what the other person did and said. We think thoughts such as: "They are at fault" or "If they would change, the situation would get better." Drawing near to God means to set the problems aside and seek God. Seek Him in prayer. This doesn't mean picking up the phone to complain to someone else. Instead, we should get on our knees and spend time near His throne of grace. Our eyes, trust, and focus need to be placed on God. We need to draw near to Him.

Fourth, seek cleansing. "Cleanse your hands, you sinners, and purify your hearts, you double-minded" (James 4:8). In the midst of a quarrel and fight, we believe we are in the right and the other parties are in the wrong. We justify what we did, and we can clearly see the wrongs of others. That is our default thinking. Remember that in a conflict, everyone contributes to it. What God is saying through this command is for us to seek cleansing. We need brokenness before a Holy God. Confess to God and to our brothers our wrong actions, words, thoughts, and motivations. There is only going to be healing in our relationships when we seek cleansing. Being double-minded is when Christians say they believe God's way, but follow worldly practices instead.

Fifth, we need to mourn and weep. "Be wretched and mourn and weep. Let your laughter be turned to mourning and your joy to gloom" (James 4:9). We tend to treat sin too lightly, even to crack jokes about it. Sin is serious, and one mark of true humility is facing the seriousness of sin and dealing with our disobedience. "A broken and contrite heart, O God, you will not despise" (Ps. 51:17). See the progression? We need to move from focusing on what other people have done to us to what we have done. Then we need to be broken for our sin. Our sin hurts people and saddens our holy God. Is our repentance a brief "I am sorry" and we move on back into the fight? Or is it real sorrow and brokenness, perhaps even with tears? What does God expect? "But this is the one to whom I will look: he who is humble and contrite in spirit and trembles at my word" (Isa. 66:2).

Sixth, humble yourself: "Humble yourselves before the Lord, and he will exalt you" (James 4:10). If we are going to have victory over quarrels and fights, we need to humble ourselves. In a fight we are filled with grandiose thoughts about ourselves. God hates the sin of pride. He will chasten the proud believer until he is humbled. Humility is agreeing with God. We are not a big deal; He is the big deal. His will must be done on earth, not my will be done in the conflict. Very powerful words were spoken by John the Baptist that must become our words: "He must increase, but I must decrease" (John 3:30). We need to be willing to set aside stubbornness and pride.

Closer Walk magazine tells the tragic story of what happens when our pride blinds us.

> *In the summer of 1986, two ships collided in the Black Sea. Hundreds of passengers died as they were hurled into the icy waters below. News of the disaster was further darkened when an investigation revealed the cause of the accident. It wasn't a technology problem like radar malfunction—or even thick fog. The cause was human stubbornness. Each captain was aware of the other ship's presence nearby. Both could have steered clear, but according to news reports, neither captain wanted to give way to the other. Each was too proud to yield first. By the time they came to their senses, it was too late.*[40]

While the pride of those captains caused the death of many others, the collateral damage of our pride is often our relationships, our ministries, and even outreach to the unsaved. Is your pride really worth that cost?

Seventh and finally, we must not speak evil to another.

> *Do not speak evil against one another, brothers. The one who speaks against a brother or judges his brother, speaks evil against the law and judges the law. But if you judge the law,*

> *you are not a doer of the law but a judge. There is only one lawgiver and judge, he who is able to save and to destroy. But who are you to judge your neighbor?*
>
> *James 4:11-12*

Picking up the phone and talking down on a brother must stop. Putting negative messages on social media and being unkind to a sister must stop. We must stop speaking evil against one another because it makes problems grow and sows division. We don't make good judges in conflict because we are only aware of part of the whole conflict. If you work in an organization and you have a problem with someone else, lateral comments to others are gossip and erode unity. Speak to the person who hurt you. If that doesn't work, share your need for help up the chain of command. Those are the folks who are there to help.

I know we covered a lot of ground, so let's take a moment to review. James 4 begins with a question: "What causes quarrels and what causes fights among you?" The answer is the world, the flesh, and the devil. What can we do when we find ourselves in a fight? Submit to God, resist the devil, draw near to God, seek cleansing, mourn and weep, humble yourself, and do not speak evil of another. If we obey these instructions, then God will draw near, cleanse us, and forgive us, and the fight will be resolved. Sometimes mental battles produce quarrels and fights, and sometimes quarrels and fights produce mental battles. Following God's instruction in James 4 will help us have victory in both.

Much more can be said about conflict resolution, but I would like to close with another important principle in resolving quarrels: Move toward the problem. Years ago I was taking a class on conflict resolution, and my professor, Dr. James Clark, told a story that highlighted this principle in a beautiful way. Some years earlier, as a pastor, Dr. Clark found himself in conflict with the chairman of his church. He was attending seminary at the time and decided to discuss the matter with his professor. After explaining to him that he was avoiding the chairman and that they were not speaking to each other except for an occasional greeting, the professor said to him, "I have one thing to tell you." Dr. Clark waited for his words of wisdom. He then said, "You have to move toward your problem!" That was a hard pill to swallow. The professor was saying Dr. Clark had to make the first move. From his perspective, the chairman was out of line and should make the first move. However, as Dr. Clark left his professor's office and headed back to the church, he understood that he had to initiate the first move in resolving their differences. That step began changing the relationship between Dr. Clark and the chairman.[41] This is a very powerful principle that can begin the process of improving relationships. Do you need to move toward your problem?

Resolving Disappointments

Early missionaries to the Marshall Islands in the central Pacific received their mail once a year when the sailing boat made its rounds of the South Pacific. On one occasion the boat was one day ahead of schedule, and the missionaries were off on a neighboring island. The captain left the mail with the Marshallese people while he attended to matters of getting stores of water and provisions. At last, the Marshallese were in possession of what the missionaries spoke about so often and apparently cherished so much. The people examined the mail to find out what was so attractive about it. They concluded that it must be good to eat, and so they proceeded to tear all the letters into tiny pieces and cook them. However, they didn't taste very good, and the Marshallese were still puzzled about the missionaries' strange interest in mail when the missionaries returned to find an entire year's worth of correspondence made into mush. If your only contact with the outside world was now another year away, this would be a huge disappointment.[42]

Everyone experiences disappointments in life. Some of those are very painful, and there is no exception for those involved in ministry. The key question is: What do you do with life's disappointments? The Oxford dictionary says that a disappointment is the feeling of sadness or displeasure caused by the defeat of one's hopes or expectations. It can also be a sense of unhappiness because someone has behaved badly toward you.[43]

People can experience a variety of hurtful disappointments: in their childhood, in marriage, at work, with a prodigal child, at church, with their health, in a financial crisis, throughout the passing of a loved one, etc. This world is not divided between people who experience disappointments and those who do not. This world is divided between people who are able to resolve their disappointments and those who are not. The ability to resolve disappointments in one's heart is of extreme importance and significantly impacts a person's quality of life. My hope is that as you read this chapter, God will help you to identify unresolved disappointments in your life so that you will experience resolution of those disappointments.

Joseph's brothers

There is a powerful account of Joseph's story in the book of Genesis that illustrates this principle. In this account, Joseph's brothers did not resolve their disappointments, but Joseph did. First, let's look at Joseph's brothers. Jacob, the family patriarch, had a house full of children. Growing up, Joseph's brothers experienced several disappointments.

- Joseph was a tattletale. He used to reveal to their father what the brothers were up to (Gen. 37:2), and they did not like that.
- Joseph was his father's favorite. Jacob loved Joseph more than the other sons and gave Joseph a special robe of many colors (Gen. 37:3).

- Joseph had special dreams, and so his brothers "hated him even more for his dreams and for his words" (Gen. 37:8).
- Jacob's special treatment of Joseph caused the brothers to be very jealous of him (Gen. 37:11).

One day Jacob sent Joseph to check on his brothers, who were keeping the sheep in Dothan. When the brothers saw Joseph, they began to conspire to kill him (Gen. 37:18). When a caravan of Ishmaelites came by, the brothers decided to sell Joseph to them as a slave (Gen. 37:28). They put an animal's blood on Joseph's robe of many colors and lied to their father, implying that Joseph was dead (Gen. 37:31).

The brothers made some terrible decisions: betrayal, attempted murder, selling their brother into slavery, deceiving their father, and breaking their father's heart. What caused the brothers to make these terrible decisions? Some of the same factors that cause Christians to make terrible decisions. Unresolved disappointments can lead to very strong negative emotions. Do you live with strong negative emotions? That could be a sign of unresolved disappointments.

Joseph's brothers resented Joseph. They became bitter. Jealousy led to hatred. Strong negative emotions eventually led to bad decisions. Unresolved disappointments can stay with people for years, even decades. The brothers' negative emotions stayed with them for many years. For example, their guilt never left them. Many years later when circumstances turned against them, "…they said to one another, 'In truth we are guilty concerning our brother, in that we saw the distress of his soul, when he begged us and we did not listen. That is why this distress has come upon us'" (Gen. 42:21).

This dark path they chose started with unresolved disappointments. Decades later, when their father died, the brothers said, "'It may be that Joseph will hate us and pay us back for all the evil that we did to him…'" (Gen. 50:15). The brothers' unresolved disappointments led to a lifetime of fear and guilt. Unfortunately, this can happen in our lives today. When disappointments are not resolved in our hearts, they can lead to bitterness and resentment, bad decisions, or guilt and deep sadness.

Joseph

Let's turn our attention to Joseph, who also experienced many severe disappointments. Let's remember Joseph's disappointments:

- Joseph heard the brothers talking about taking his life.
- Joseph was thrown into a pit by his brothers.
- Joseph was sold as a slave by his own brothers and taken to Egypt, far from his family.
- He was sold a second time to Potiphar, an officer of Pharaoh, the captain of the guard (Gen. 39:1).
- While there, Potiphar's wife lied about Joseph, and Joseph went to prison having done nothing wrong (Gen. 39:20).
- Joseph asked Pharaoh's chief cupbearer to mention his plight to the king. Despite Joseph's help given to the now-released prisoner, he was forgotten and left behind (Gen. 40:23).

Did you notice that Joseph's disappointments seemed to be much more severe than those of his brothers? He ended up removed from his family by force, became a slave, and spent about 12 years in prison unjustly. If there was someone who had a reason to be resentful, it was Joseph. But he chose not to harbor that resentment. Let's review the account. Joseph interpreted Pharaoh's dreams and was made the second in command in all of Egypt. In the years of hunger, Jacob sent some of his sons to Egypt to buy food. There the brothers encountered Joseph. On a second trip to Egypt, all the brothers were together, including the youngest and Joseph's only full brother, Benjamin. Joseph revealed himself to his brothers. Now Joseph had the power to make his brothers pay for what they did to him, but he did not. Why? The answer is simple. With God's help, Joseph had resolved his disappointments in his heart long before this moment. If Joseph was able to resolve his disappointments with the Lord's help, so can we. So can you. Let's take a look at Joseph to learn from him how we can resolve disappointments in our lives.

1. Recognize the wrong that was done to you, but don't make that your permanent dwelling.

Joseph didn't pretend his hurtful past hadn't happened. He spoke honestly to Pharaoh's cupbearer: "I was indeed stolen out of the land of the Hebrews, and here also I have done nothing that they should put me into the pit" (Gen. 40:15). In order to heal from your disappointments, you need to recognize that they happened and that they are hurtful. There is a time to grieve those hurts, but you also need to make the decision that you are not going to live there permanently. It is healthy to move on and heal from that disappointment.

After Joseph became prime minister in Egypt, he got married and had children. It is interesting to notice what he called his sons. Back in those days, personal names had special meanings. "Joseph called the name of the firstborn Manasseh. 'For,' he said, 'God has made me forget all my hardship and all my father's house.' The name of the second he called Ephraim, 'For God has made me fruitful in the land of my affliction'" (Gen. 41:51-52). Joseph recognized his hurt, but he saw that God was helping him forget his hardship and that God was bringing good things into his life despite the afflictions he had suffered.

We, too, need to recognize the pain that was caused in our lives, but we must decide to look to God for healing from those past hurts and for better things in our lives. We must decide not to live in the past. When we live in the past, we miss the good that God is bringing to our lives today and into the future.

2. Focus on your daily relationship with God, not on the injustice done to you.

When people are hurt, they eventually need to decide to stop focusing on the situation, stop licking their wounds, and instead focus on God and His Word. What was Joseph's focus? We read about Joseph walking with God and talking about God in Genesis 39:2: "The Lord was with Joseph...." In Genesis 39:21 we read, "But the Lord was with Joseph...." Others could see that Joseph walked with God. They did not see God physically standing next to Joseph, but other people can tell that a person walks with God by their actions and by their words.

Even Pharaoh could see that Joseph walked with God: "Pharaoh said to his servants, "Can we find a man like this, in whom is the Spirit of God?" (Gen. 41:38). We need to choose to focus on God and walk with Him each day. Let God speak to your heart through His Word and heal your soul. Lift your eyes from your disappointments to the God who is able to work good things out of any disappointment. He is the God who brings new life out of the valley of dry bones (Ezek. 37). Focus on Him. Pursue Him. Joseph walked with God even in prison; follow his example. Seek God in the prison of your disappointments, and He will surely set you free.

3. Focus on pleasing God, not yourself.

Sometimes we rationalize that we can seek some kind of pleasure in things because, after all, we have been hurt. At times we even know those things will end up hurting us. So many Christians with unresolved disappointments turn to substance abuse, addictions, or unhealthy relationships. They are trying to numb the pain. That is deceptive thinking. We need to decide that we are only going to seek the things that please God.

After Joseph was rejected by his brothers, he found himself in a new country where his boss's wife kept pursuing him. Joseph could have rationalized this pleasure for a moment. He was far from home, and no one in his family would find out. He had been rejected by his brothers and now was in front of a woman who was accepting him. Instead, Joseph decided to please God above all others, including himself, and he told her no. He said, "How then can I do this great wickedness and sin against God?" (Gen. 39:9). When we've been hurt by disappointments, we need to make decisions based on what is pleasing to God and not to ourselves. We need to turn to God and ask Him to meet the needs of our hearts instead of turning to the things of the world to seek to meet those needs.

4. Forgive and love those who hurt you.

Later Joseph was in a perfect place for revenge against his brothers, yet he chose to forgive and love his brothers. "But Joseph said to them, 'Do not fear, for am I in the place of God? As for you, you meant evil against me, but God meant it for good, to bring it about that many people should be kept alive, as they are today. So do not fear; I will provide for you and your little ones.' Thus he comforted them and spoke kindly to them" (Gen. 50:19-21).

This is a true sign of forgiveness. The biblical text does not indicate that Joseph ever told his father what his brothers did to him. He did not want to break his father's heart and hurt his brothers—a strong sign of forgiveness. His continual focus on God, who is forgiving and loving, led Joseph to forgive and love his brothers, even though they didn't deserve it. God has forgiven you and loves you, and He asks you to do the same to the person who disappointed you. Ask God for the grace to do just that. It doesn't come from you. It comes from God through you. As this is an important topic, we will dig deeper into the topic of forgiveness in the next chapter.

In some cases, people feel that God is the one who disappointed them. Remember that God is not the author of evil; He works even through broken things to bring about good: "…for those who love God all things work together for good…" (Rom. 8:28). The path to a better quality of life and a more fruitful ministry for you takes you through forgiveness and love. God will help you do that.

5. Speak God's truth to yourself and others.

Joseph decided not to wallow in his past hurt, but to focus on God, to walk with Him, and to trust Him. His words revealed his focus on God. Here are some examples:

- He told the Pharaoh's baker and cupbearer, "…Do not interpretations belong to God?" (Gen. 40:8).
- When Pharaoh had dreams, Joseph was called to interpret them. Joseph could have taken credit for himself to make himself look good, but instead, "Joseph answered Pharaoh, 'It is not in me; God will give Pharaoh a favorable answer'" (Gen. 41:16).
- After Joseph interpreted Pharaoh's dream, he affirmed again the source of this revelation, "…God has revealed to Pharaoh what he is about to do'" (Gen. 41:25).

Words matter! When our words are God-centered instead of self-centered, they reveal that our hearts are focusing on God and not on ourselves. Your words reveal your focus. Your heart needs to hear your own mouth speak the truths of God. God also told Joshua to do this: "This Book of the Law shall not depart from your mouth…" (Josh. 1:8). It is the truth of God's Word that corrects our faulty thinking. It is not enough to think you know key truths about God; your mouth must speak them. Your ears need to hear them so that they are absorbed into your heart and soul.

6. Trust the Sovereign heart of God and His ability to bring about good when others fail you.

When Joseph finally revealed himself to his brothers, he spoke of what God had shown him:"…do not be distressed or angry with yourselves because you sold me here, for God sent me before you to preserve life… God sent me before you to preserve for you a remnant on earth, and to keep alive for you many survivors. So, it was not you who sent me here, but God" (Gen. 45:5-8).

Perhaps one day you will see how God turned your painful disappointment into something good. He loves you, and He has good plans for you. "For I know the plans I have for you, declares the Lord, plans for welfare and not for evil, to give you a future and a hope" (Jer. 29:11). Today, perhaps, you still don't see it. Until you do, trust the sovereign heart of God and His ability to bring about good when others fail you.

When that disappointment feels contrary to what we think God would choose for His children, it's often because we don't see things from His perspective.

> *The year was 1920. The scene was the examining board for selecting missionaries. Standing before the board was a young man named Oswald Smith. One dream dominated his heart. He wanted to be a missionary. Over and over again, he prayed, "Lord, I want to go as a missionary for you. Open a door of service for me." Now, at last, his prayer would be answered. When the examination was over, the board turned Oswald Smith down. He did not meet their qualifications. He failed the test. Oswald Smith had set his direction, but now life gave him a detour. What would he do? As Oswald Smith prayed, God planted another idea in his heart. If he could not go as a missionary, he would build a church which could send out missionaries. And that is what he did. Oswald Smith pastored The People's Church in Toronto, Canada, which sent out more missionaries than any other church at that time. Oswald Smith brought God into the situation, and God transformed his detour into a main channel of service.* [44]

Are you willing to trust the sovereign heart of God and His ability to bring about good when circumstances or people fail you? Some people are able to resolve the disappointments in their hearts, make good decisions, and live a more peaceful life. Others are not able to resolve their disappointments: They bury them in their souls, they become resentful, and their own quality of life suffers. We read in Hebrews 12:15, “See to it that no one fails to obtain the grace of God; that no ‘root of bitterness’ springs up and causes trouble, and by it many become defiled.”

Many mental battles are fought in our minds, fueled by unresolved disappointments. The ability to resolve disappointments in one’s heart is of extreme importance, and it significantly impacts a person’s life, family, and ministry. Let’s learn from Joseph’s example and resolve the disappointments in your heart for the glory of God and for peace in your heart and your relationships. Do you have disappointments that need to be resolved?

Forgiveness: Dothan Revisited

In 1492, Spain expelled its Jewish population as part of the Spanish Inquisition. Tens of thousands of Spanish Jews fled to Portugal, where King John II granted them asylum in return for a cash payment. However, the asylum was only temporary—after eight months, the Portuguese government decreed the enslavement of all Jews who had not yet left the country. Following John's death in 1494, the new King Manuel I of Portugal decreed that all Jews had to convert to Christianity or leave the country without their children. Hard times followed for the Portuguese Jews, with the horrible massacre of two thousand people in Lisbon in 1506. About five hundred years later, in 2006, the Portuguese president at the time, Mário Soares, for the first time in the history of Portugal asked forgiveness of the Jewish communities of Portuguese origin for Portugal's responsibility in the Inquisition and for all the past persecutions of Jews. The Jewish community leaders were present to mark that public apology, and a special monument was dedicated to that effect. Revisiting this past very painful experience in this way was a very important step in the healing process for the current Jewish community.

Past painful experiences are a factory of mental battles in our lives. The pain caused many years ago continues to sadden our souls and affect our thoughts. I believe that healing can come when people revisit past painful experiences. It's time to revisit one of the most beautiful stories in the Bible: the story of Joseph in Genesis. In an earlier chapter, we considered the implications of his story upon our disappointments, but this is a story full of twists and turns, full of both heartbreaking and redeeming moments and also of wonder and mystery. One of the most intriguing aspects of Joseph's story is found in Genesis 42-44. As a matter of fact, for the quick reader, these chapters don't make a lot of sense. Why did Joseph not reveal himself to his brothers when they first arrived in Egypt to buy food? Was it because of revenge? Payback? I don't think so. In Genesis 45 we see that Joseph had come to understand the sovereignty of God over what had happened to him, and he knew that it was God working good out of painful situations. It is indeed a mystery why Joseph gave his brothers "the runaround" for three whole chapters in Genesis. I want to present to you why I believe Joseph did what he did.

Here is a quick review of that narrative. In Genesis 41, Joseph left prison to become the prime minister of Egypt, the person in command of Egypt after Pharaoh himself. In Genesis 42, Jacob sent his sons to Egypt to buy food. When they arrived, Joseph recognized them, but did not reveal himself to them. Genesis 42:7 says that "he treated them like strangers." Why? What did Joseph have in mind? He called them spies and put them all in prison for three days. After those three days in prison, Joseph told his brothers to leave one brother in prison in Egypt while they went to get their younger brother and bring him to Joseph. That was the only way they could prove that they were not spies. This turn of events had the brothers dialoguing among themselves as they remembered what they had done to Joseph in Dothan years earlier. The only explanation they had for this bad situation was connecting it with the guilt they had carried for years about what they did to

Joseph. "Then they said to one another, 'In truth we are guilty concerning our brother, in that we saw the distress of his soul, when he begged us and we did not listen. That is why this distress has come upon us.' And Reuben answered them, 'Did I not tell you not to sin against the boy? But you did not listen. So now there comes a reckoning for his blood'" (Gen. 42:21-22). To make things worse, Simeon was put in shackles before their eyes.

The brothers returned home to Canaan. They told their father all that had happened. They asked Jacob to let them bring Benjamin to Egypt, and then Simeon would bring him back home. Jacob responded, "My son shall not go down with you, for his brother is dead, and he is the only one left. If harm should happen to him on the journey that you are to make, you would bring down my gray hairs with sorrow to Sheol" (Gen. 42:38).

Genesis 43 reveals that life was going well until Jacob's household food stock began to run low. Jacob told his children, "Go again, buy us a little food" (Gen. 43:2). Jacob's children reminded their father that the man in Egypt told them that if they did not bring Benjamin to Egypt with them, they would not see his face. Judah promised his father Benjamin's safety if Jacob would agree to let him go to Egypt. Finally, Jacob agreed to let Benjamin go and told his children, "May God Almighty grant you mercy before the man, and may he send back your other brother and Benjamin. And as for me, if I am bereaved of my children, I am bereaved" (Gen. 43:14).

When they arrived in Egypt, Joseph invited all the brothers for a meal at his house. Perhaps this would be a great place for Joseph to reveal himself to his brothers. He became emotional, but he did not reveal himself to his brothers then. Whatever moment Joseph had been looking for, he had not yet found. What was Joseph waiting for?

In Genesis 44, Jacob's sons were sent home with the food they came for. They were all together again. It felt like a mission accomplished, and they thought their father would be glad. Early in the journey, however, they were stopped by Joseph's servants. The cup of the prime minister of Egypt had gone missing. To that accusation the brothers responded confidently, "Whichever of your servants is found with it shall die, and we also will be my lord's servants" (Gen. 44:9). Joseph's servant responded, "Let it be as you say: he who is found with it shall be my servant, and the rest of you shall be innocent" (Gen. 44:10). As the bags were opened, the cup was in Benjamin's bag. "They tore their clothes" and returned to the city.

After being confronted by Joseph, Judah said, "…behold, we are my lord's servants, both we and he also in whose hand the cup has been found" (Gen 44:16). Joseph responded, "…Only the man in whose hand the cup was found shall be my servant. But as for you, go up in peace to your father" (Gen. 44:17). At that critical moment, Judah asked Egypt's prime minister for permission to speak. Judah took leadership in that critical moment and said in Genesis 44:30-34:

> *Now therefore, as soon as I come to your servant my father, and the boy is not with us, then, as his life is bound up in the boy's life, as soon as he sees that the boy is not with us, he will die, and your servants will bring down the gray hairs of your servant our father with sorrow to Sheol. For your servant became a pledge of safety for the boy to my father, saying, "If I do not bring him back to you, then I shall bear the blame before my father all my life." Now therefore, please let your*

servant remain instead of the boy as a servant to my lord, and let the boy go back with his brothers. For how can I go back to my father if the boy is not with me? I fear to see the evil that would find my father.

Notice how Judah stepped up as a leader and how, as the brother who was in the lineage of the Savior, he offered to take Benjamin's place—a foreshadowing of what Christ would do later for us. We are now at the end of Genesis 44. For three full chapters, Joseph has been interacting with his brothers and has yet to reveal himself to them. I think this was the moment that Joseph had been working toward. You see, Joseph wanted to revisit Dothan.

Dothan is the place where Joseph's brothers wanted to kill him. They threw him into a pit and sold him as slave to be separated from his family for about 25 years. I call this moment "Dothan revisited." Notice the number of elements that are so similar between the Dothan event in Genesis 37 and the Egypt event in Genesis 44:

- In Dothan they were away from Jacob. In Egypt they were away from Jacob again.
- In Dothan the younger brother was Joseph. In Egypt the younger brother was Benjamin.
- In Dothan the younger brother was going to the pit. In Egypt the younger brother was going to prison.
- In Dothan the destiny of Joseph was in the hands of all the brothers. In Egypt the destiny of all the brothers was in the hands of Joseph.

I believe that, in recreating Dothan in Egypt, Joseph was looking to find out if his brothers had changed since Dothan. Had they matured? Had they grown? Were they now merciful and kind? Let's continue to notice the parallels, but also the changes in his brothers:

- In Dothan the brothers did not care that the younger brother, Joseph, would not be returning home. This would break their father's heart. In Egypt the brothers were very concerned for their father and what would happen to him if the younger brother, Benjamin, did not return home.
- In Dothan they didn't care as the younger brother cried for mercy. In Egypt they were concerned for the younger brother.

The brothers had changed. God had done a work in their hearts. I believe Joseph wanted to revisit that scene all over again. What he saw in his brothers is what he had hoped to have seen in them 25 years earlier in Dothan. Joseph was reliving the story, and this time he saw his brothers do the right thing. The cruelty displayed 25 years earlier now became mercy, compassion, and kindness. With this realization Joseph's heart was full, and suddenly his eyes became full of tears. As Genesis 45 begins, he says, "Make everyone go out from here" (Gen. 45:1).

The climax of these three chapters in Genesis was Joseph realizing his brothers had changed. Once that happened, he was ready to reveal himself. "And he wept aloud, so that the Egyptians heard it, and the household of Pharaoh heard it. And Joseph said to his brothers, "I am Joseph! Is my father still alive?" But his brothers could not answer him, for they were dismayed at his presence" (Gen. 45:2-3). He continued to speak to his brothers, "…I am your brother, Joseph, whom you sold into Egypt…. God sent me before you to preserve for you a remnant on earth, and to keep alive for you many survivors. So it was not you who sent me here, but

God…" (Gen. 45:4, 7-8). What beautiful and powerful words. Those are words that reveal Joseph had forgiven his brothers.

I am telling you this story because Joseph had a very painful experience in his life that needed to be revisited so he could experience full healing. He needed closure so that he could let go and so that his brothers could experience redemption. How about you? Is there a painful experience in your past that perhaps needs revisiting? Perhaps it is a painful family experience, or perhaps it is a painful ministry experience. God wants you to revisit your Dothan incident and experience healing, forgiveness, and redemption. Most of the time the only way to experience healing from a past painful experience is to forgive those who hurt you.

Our God is a forgiving God. "The Lord our God is merciful and forgiving, even though we have rebelled against him" (Dan. 9:9). As Christians, we have been forgiven. God expects us to extend the forgiveness we have received to those who have offended us. "Bearing with one another and, if one has a complaint against another, forgiving each other; as the Lord has forgiven you, so you also must forgive" (Col. 3:13). This verse and others say that forgiveness for the Christian is mandatory because we have been forgiven. Christians should be known as the people who forgive. It is who we are; it is our identity.

Evangelical pastor, teacher, and author Chuck Swindoll reports that a seminary student in Chicago faced a forgiveness test. Although he preferred to work in some kind of ministry, the only job he could find was driving a bus on Chicago's South Side. One day a gang of tough teens got on board and refused to pay the fare. After a few days of this, the seminarian spotted a policeman on the corner, stopped the bus, and reported them. The officer made them pay, but then he got off. When the bus rounded a corner, the gang robbed the seminarian and beat him severely. He pressed charges, and the gang was rounded up. They were found guilty. But as soon as the jail sentence was given, the young Christian saw their spiritual need and felt pity for them. So he asked the judge if he could serve their sentences for them. The gang members and the judge were dumbfounded. "It's because I forgive you," he explained. His request was denied, but he visited the young men in jail and led several of them to faith in Christ.[45]

Christian counselor and author June Hunt said, "It takes two for reconciliation, only one for forgiveness."[46] It is very difficult to achieve victory over mental battles if you carry unforgiveness in your heart. Hunt explains why it is important to rid yourself of unforgiveness:

> *When you refuse to forgive, your unforgiveness keeps you emotionally stuck to both the offense and the offender. A continual refusal to forgive digs a deeper hole in which you can easily hide your hardened heart. Your past hurts, though buried, are still very much alive. And because they are not released in God's way, oddly enough, you become like your offender (but you are blind to it). Not forgiving your offender is an offense to God, thereby making you an offender to God as well!* [47]

An offense in your life that you are unwilling to forgive will eventually become a spiritual stronghold. This can become a foothold for the enemy to launch attacks on you. "'In your anger do not sin': Do not let the sun go down while you are still angry, and do not give the devil a foothold" (Eph. 4:26-27). A foothold will become a source of spiritual warfare. The good news is that a spiritual stronghold can be defeated.

Before we talk about an important prayer of deliverance, I want to share a powerful true story. In 1910 Japan invaded, conquered, and occupied Korea for 35 years. When they arrived, they boarded up the evangelical churches and ejected most foreign missionaries. They were ruthless to the Korean population. They refused to allow churches to meet and jailed many key Christian spokesmen. One pastor persistently pleaded with his local Japanese police chief for permission to meet for services. His nagging was finally accommodated, and the police chief offered to unlock his church—for one meeting.

Long before dawn on that promised Sunday, Korean families throughout a wide area made their way to the church. It was during a stanza of "Nearer, My God, to Thee" that the Japanese police chief waiting outside gave the orders. The people toward the back of the church could hear them when they barricaded the doors, but no one realized that they had doused the church with kerosene until they smelled the smoke. The dried wood structure of the small church quickly ignited. Realizing the end was near, with a calm that comes from confidence, the pastor led his congregation in the hymn "At the Cross," and its words served as a fitting farewell to earth and a loving salutation to heaven. With smoke burning their eyes, their song became a serenade to the horrified and helpless witnesses outside.

Clearing the incinerated remains was the easy part. Erasing the hate would take many, many years. In the decades that followed, that bitterness was passed on to a new generation. Bitterness clamps down on your soul like iron shackles. The Korean people who found it too hard to forgive could not enjoy the "peace that passes all understanding." Hatred choked their joy. No hope came until 1972, when a group of Japanese pastors traveling through Korea came upon a memorial. When they read the details of the tragedy and the names of the spiritual brothers and sisters who had perished, they were overcome with shame.

They returned to Japan committed to right a wrong. With their fellow believers they raised 10 million yen ($25,000). The money was transferred through proper channels, and a beautiful white church building was erected on the site of the tragedy. When the dedication service for the new building was held, a delegation from Japan joined the relatives and special guests. Although their generosity was acknowledged and their attempts at making peace appreciated, the memories were still there. Hatred preserves pain. It keeps the wounds open and the hurts fresh.

The speeches were made, the details of the tragedy recalled, and the names of the dead honored. When the song leader began the words to "Nearer, My God, to Thee," something remarkable happened as the voices mingled on the familiar melody. As the memories of the past mixed with the truth of the song, resistance started to melt. The song leader closed the service with the hymn "At the Cross." The normally stoic Japanese could not contain themselves. They turned to their Korean spiritual relatives and begged them to forgive. The guarded, calloused hearts of the Koreans were not quick to surrender. But the love of the Japanese believers tore at the Koreans' emotions. "At the cross, at the cross, where I first saw the light, and the burden of my heart rolled away...." One Korean turned toward a Japanese brother, then another. And then the floodgates holding back a wave of emotion let go. They clung to each other and wept. Japanese tears of repentance and Korean tears of forgiveness intermingled to bathe the site of an old nightmare.[48]

Healing can come when God helps us to revisit past painful experiences. Joseph had a very painful experience in his life that needed to be revisited so that he could experience true healing and his brothers could experience redemption. How about you? Perhaps God wants you to revisit your Dothan incident and experience healing, forgiveness, and redemption. June Hunt in her book *How to Forgive When You Don't Feel Like It* presents a spiritual warfare prayer to help you to honestly confront and release your angry, unforgiving heart and experience true forgiveness. If you are ready to revisit your Dothan now, then pray this prayer out loud.

Spiritual Warfare Prayer:

Dear Heavenly Father,
I don't want to be defeated in my life. Thank You that Jesus, who lives in me, is greater than Satan, who is in the world (1 John 4:4).

I know I have been bought with the price of Christ's blood, which was shed at Calvary. My body is not my own — it belongs to Christ (1 Cor. 6:19-20.).

Right now, I refuse all thoughts that are not from You (2 Cor. 10:3-5).

I choose to forgive those who have hurt me, and I choose to release all of my pain and anger into Your hands (Col. 3:13).

I resist Satan and all his power (James 4:7).

As I stand in the full armor of God, I ask You to bind Satan and his demonic forces from having any influence over me (Eph. 6:11).

From now on, with the shield of faith, I will deflect and defeat every unforgiving thought that could defeat me (Eph. 6:16).

And I yield my life to Your plan and Your purpose (Jer. 29:11).

In the holy name of Jesus I pray. Amen.[49]

The Original Mental Battle

In the beginning of time, circumstances were perfect. There was plenty of food, rest, and relaxation. Life was good. God would show up in the garden that He had created on a regular basis to fellowship with Adam and Eve. Can you imagine? They had face-to-face conversations with the Creator of the Universe! That must have been amazing! Adam and Eve had each other's company with animals to observe, a serene river to enjoy, and delicious fruit from many trees, and all of this was in an absolutely beautiful garden. The work to maintain the garden was enjoyable and purposeful. All was well.

In this garden there was only one rule they had to keep. Can you even count how many rules and laws you and I need to be mindful of? Rules at school, rules at work, driving laws, IRS laws, subdivision rules, rules at home, rules in an airplane, rules in parks, rules at the beach, etc. We live under hundreds of rules and laws every day of our lives. What would it feel like if you lived under one rule or commandment? It sounds amazing. This was the one commandment Adam and Eve received: "And the Lord God commanded the man, saying, 'You may surely eat of every tree of the garden, but of the tree of the knowledge of good and evil you shall not eat, for in the day that you eat of it you shall surely die'" (Genesis 2:16-17). That seemed pretty simple. There was one rule, and the consequences were clear. There was no confusion. Since there were hundreds of trees with delicious fruit, there was no need to eat from the tree God had forbidden. This one rule was simple, and it was not difficult to abide by it. Life was good.

Then the serpent entered the stage. The serpent brought an anti-God message. The serpent was very smart, very cunning, and very crafty. The devil was speaking through this serpent. We know that because later, when God described to the serpent the consequences of its evil actions, God said, "I will put enmity between you and the woman, and between your offspring and her offspring; he shall bruise your head, and you shall bruise his heel" (Gen. 3:15). This is a prophetic word from God. The offspring of the woman would be Christ. The offspring of the serpent is Satan. Satan would bruise Christ's heel, which would not be a mortal injury. Christ would bruise Satan's head, which referenced a mortal injury. Christ would be victorious over Satan in the end. This prophecy is also an encouragement to us today. Yes, we will have mental battles, but in the end, Satan is defeated and Christ is victorious. We are on the side of victory! What we learn about that first mental battle is going to help us in our own mental battles. This is precisely how Satan has access to the believer. He plants thoughts in our minds, but that is the extent of his access. Satan cannot possess Christians, for we are indwelled by the Holy Spirit. We are going to look at how this battle happened and consider its several aspects.

The Message: The serpent starts dialoguing with the woman. "He said to the woman, 'Did God actually say, 'You shall not eat of any tree in the garden'?" (Gen. 3:1). It all starts with a message sent from the serpent to the woman. The serpent initiates the mental battle.

The Doubt: The first idea the serpent plants in Eve's mind is doubt. "He said to the woman, 'Did God actually say, "You shall not eat of any tree in the garden'?" (Gen. 3:1). In other words: "Eve, did you hear correctly? Did God actually say that? Did God really mean that?" That seed of doubt triggered interest for more conversation. It invited a response from Eve.

The Dialogue: Eve responded by restating what God had said: "And the woman said to the serpent, 'We may eat of the fruit of the trees in the garden, but God said, "You shall not eat of the fruit of the tree that is in the midst of the garden, neither shall you touch it, lest you die" (Gen. 3:2-3). Eve responded by speaking truth to the serpent, but she added something that God had not said: "Neither shall you touch it." Anytime we start dialoguing with the enemy, the truth starts changing. This is where the conversation should have stopped. She should have said, "That is all there is to be said. You need to go now." Satan had accomplished his first goal: He was now dialoguing with Eve. The communication lines were now open.

The Lie: Now that the dialogue was open and a seed of doubt had been planted in Eve, the serpent continued: "But the serpent said to the woman, 'You will not surely die. For God knows that when you eat of it your eyes will be opened, and you will be like God, knowing good and evil'" (Gen. 3:4-5). The serpent lied to Eve. The serpent contradicted what God said, saying, "You will not die." The serpent went on to explain that God had hidden motives and was not being truthful.

The Amazing Offer: The serpent said that wonderful things would happen when Eve would eat of the fruit of the tree in the midst of the garden.

1. "Your eyes will be opened." Eve would have new understanding and insight.
2. "You will be like God." Adam and Eve were amazed at the magnificent God they fellowshipped with. They could be just like Him? Wow!
3. You will know "good and evil." The tree of good and evil was a bit of a mystery to them. God had told them not to eat of the tree of the knowledge of good and evil, but he did not explain more about this mystery. Now they would be able to know all things about it. Adam and Eve did not know what evil was.

They were intrigued by this amazing offer. They felt good about it. This made sense to them. Temptations are designed to make sense to the one tempted. The Great Wall of China is a gigantic structure that cost an immense amount of money and labor to build. When it was finished, it appeared impregnable. But the enemy breached it, not by breaking it down or going around it. They did it by bribing the gatekeepers. Human hearts are easily deceived. It was that way with the guards of the Great Wall of China, and it was that way with Adam and Eve.

The Decision: The information was good, the offer was good, and it felt right, so they made the decision to act based on the newly acquired information. "So when the woman saw that the tree was good for food, and that it was a delight to the eyes, and that the tree was to be desired to make one wise, she took of its fruit and ate, and she also gave some to her husband who was with her, and he ate" (Genesis 3:6). Consider the basis for this decision.

1. The tree was good for food.
2. It was a delight to the eyes.

3. The tree was to be desired to make one wise.

Adam and Eve were fighting a mental battle. What we know of their thoughts reveals how far they strayed from the words that God said. Their thinking is very messed up, and their emotions are strong. Look at the words they use: "good," "delight," "desired." Wrong thinking leads to wrong emotions, and those lead to wrong decisions. They ate of the fruit, and they disobeyed God. They had only one rule, and they broke it. John Piper says that sin "gets its power by persuading me to believe that I will be more happy if I follow it. The power of all temptation is the prospect that it will make me happier."[50]

The Consequences: You can pick your decision, but you cannot pick the consequences. Those will be picked for you. "Then the eyes of both were opened, and they knew that they were naked. And they sewed fig leaves together and made themselves loincloths" (Gen. 3:7). The first consequence was shame. The second consequence was guilt. "And they heard the sound of the Lord God walking in the garden in the cool of the day, and the man and his wife hid themselves from the presence of the Lord God among the trees of the garden" (Gen. 3:8). In the past, when they heard God walking in the garden, they ran to Him to visit with Him. Now they ran away from Him to hide themselves. Shame and guilt had started separating them from God. It is the same way today. When Christians live in sin, they don't talk to God, they don't open God's Word, they don't go to church, and they don't want to talk about the Lord with other believers. Guilt and shame take over their hearts.

Genesis 3:8-23 tells us about God's conversation with Adam and Eve. Verse 12 tells us that Adam was not ready to own up to the fact that he also ate from the fruit, so he accused Eve, saying that it was her fault. Of course, Eve didn't own up to her decision either, so she accused the serpent in verse 13. Finally, with no one else to blame, God started issuing consequences to them, beginning with the serpent.

- The serpent will be cursed, crawl on his belly, and eat dust, and the serpent's head will be bruised by the offspring of the woman (vv. 14-15).
- The woman will have pain in childbearing and be in submission to Adam (v. 16). Adam will have hardship in work (v. 17). Death will occur (v. 19). Removal from the garden, which meant separation from God, follows (v. 24).

Through the rest of the book of Genesis and the entire Bible, we realize that the consequences of Adam and Eve's disobedience to God are brutal, and they pass on from generation to generation. Yet, the Lord is a merciful God, and in Genesis 3:15 He promises that the seed of the woman, Christ, would undo the works of Satan and make a way for the human rebellion to be forgiven.

Let's think about us today. When your mind tells you that the temptation looks really good, remind yourself of what life will look like if you decide to follow through. Insects are often drawn to an Australian plant known as the sundew. Just as our temptations may be enticing, these bugs see the sundew's beautiful flower and delicate leaves as a great attraction. That temptation returns with harsh consequences for the bug, though, as the sticky leaves trap him, closing around him before he is devoured.[51] Even though the temptation is attractive, there are definite consequences that are easy to forget or ignore. What are the consequences for choosing that beautiful bait in front of you?

The pattern of mental battles that we see in Genesis 3 is the pattern repeated countless times in our lives. The message. The doubt. The dialogue. The lie. The amazing offer. The decision. The consequences. If we are going to stop it before damage is done, we must stop it at the beginning. We have no business welcoming messages from the enemy and then thinking about them. Jesus taught us to say, "Be gone, Satan" (Matt. 4:10) and "Get behind me, Satan" (Matt. 16:23). The enemy is so cunning that we cannot outsmart him. It starts with him placing an idea in our heads. He sends us a message. Right there we need to reject it out loud: "No, I don't accept this. I reject this. I will not allow this kind of message in my head." Benjamin Franklin said, "It is easier to suppress the first desire than to satisfy all that follow it." Eve's response to the serpent was this: "We may eat of the fruit of the trees in the garden, but God said, 'You shall not eat of the fruit of the tree that is in the midst of the garden, neither shall you touch it, lest you die.'" But what if she would have added, "You need to leave, or I will leave. We are done talking"? There would have been a very different outcome. Or perhaps Eve could have stopped the dialogue and gone to ask God what He thought about the words from the serpent and how to respond to the serpent.

The mental battles that we experience in life seem to be external to us. We pass blame to others or say it was because of this circumstance or that incident. We say: My environment, my community, my society, my company, or my church was at fault. We see the world as "out there, causing me problems." I don't think this is the truth. We interact with the world around us with our minds. The major problem is not external to us. Look at Adam and Eve. They were surrounded with perfection. Everything was just right, yet their minds got them into a mental battle that led them to choose to disobey God. The consequences came rushing in as their quality of life went down the tubes. It is the same thing today. In my travels around the country and around the world, I have met people who have very little or who have great trials in their lives, but they have the joy of the Lord in their hearts and the peace of God in their minds. I have also met those who seem to have everything except joy and peace. I don't think the key is perfect circumstances around us. I think the key is how our mind engages with the circumstances around us. Because the tempter is still present, we will experience mental battles. God's Word gives us instructions for how to have victory over mental battles. Christ is always victorious. As we walk close to Him, we will experience His victory. While in this earthly, fallen, unredeemed body, we will lose mental battles from time to time. But one day, at our glorification, all mental battles will end.

> In order to have victory in our mental battles and break the cycle (the message, the doubt, the dialogue, the lie, the amazing offer, the decision, and the consequences), we need to push away the lie, refuse to dialogue, and occupy our mind with good things. "Finally, brothers, whatever is true, whatever is honorable, whatever is just, whatever is pure, whatever is lovely, whatever is commendable, if there is any excellence, if there is anything worthy of praise, think about these things. What you have learned and received and heard and seen in me—practice these things, and the God of peace will be with you" (Phil. 4:8-9). Right thinking ultimately leads to good decisions, and the result is the peace of God in our hearts. What can you do to experience victory in your mental battles?

Resist the Devil and He Will Flee from You

Years ago, a coworker walked into my office in tears. I asked, "What happened?" She went on to tell me that a pastor she knew on the East Coast had been caught in adultery and lost his ministry. A few weeks later, he took his life. My friend was in shock by what had taken place and heartbroken over the pain left in the pastor's family, the congregation, and the community. After we prayed together and she left my office, I was left reflecting. In order for this pastor to make this series of bad decisions, he had likely been immersed in serious mental battles for a long time. Unfortunately, we have all read similar stories of when people in ministry make very bad decisions. There are times when the mental battles take on a severe intensity, and there is an intense darkness and oppression that assails the servant of God. I believe God gave us special instruction to deal with those battles. It is summarized in the words "resist the devil."

In personal conflicts, so many times we think that it is a particular person who is making our life difficult. We must remember that our real battle is not against that person: "For we do not wrestle against flesh and blood, but against the rulers, against the authorities, against the cosmic powers over this present darkness, against the spiritual forces of evil in the heavenly places" (Eph. 6:12). The real battle is against enemies we can't see, but they are very real. The Word of God tells us that we must not be ignorant of Satan's schemes "so that we would not be outwitted by Satan; for we are not ignorant of his designs" (2 Cor. 2:11). Our focus needs to be on learning about God, but at the same time to have a basic knowledge of what the Scriptures teach about the workings of the enemy of our souls.

There is a command to Christians in the New Testament that is quite thought-provoking. It is the command for us to resist the devil. "Submit yourselves to God. Resist the devil, and he will flee from you" (James 4:7). This same command also appears in 1 Peter 5:8-9: "Be self-controlled and alert. Your enemy the devil prowls around like a roaring lion looking for someone to devour. Resist him, standing firm in the faith." If God commanded us to resist the devil, it is because He expects us to resist the devil. How do we do that? It sounds like we have something to do. What must we do in practical terms to obey this commandment from God?

This issue tends to become neglected due to abuses. On one side, some Christian circles misuse this topic, and they see the devil under every rock. Other Christians tend to swing the pendulum to the other extreme and not talk about him at all. Both extremes are wrong. We need a biblical and balanced view of this topic. Before we understand how to obey this commandment from God, let's review some of the workings of the devil, as we are supposed to be aware of his schemes.

Satan is the deceiver of the world. "And the great dragon was thrown down, that ancient serpent, who is called the devil and Satan, the deceiver of the whole world…" (Rev. 12:9). Remember that God's Word teaches that humans are easily deceived. The deceiver and deceived make a bad combination. Satan is the father of lies. "You are of your father the devil, and your will is to do your father's desires. He was a murderer from the beginning, and does not stand in the truth, because there is no truth in him. When he lies, he speaks out of his own character, for he is a liar and the father of lies" (John 8:44).

We know that as Christians we are protected by God, and Satan cannot touch us. "We know that everyone who has been born of God does not keep on sinning, but he who was born of God protects him, and the evil one does not touch him" (1 John 5:18). Satan cannot possess a Christian because the Holy Spirit lives in us. What Satan can do to unbelievers is different than what he can do to believers. What can he do to unbelievers? "And you were dead in the trespasses and sins in which you once walked, following the course of this world, following the prince of the power of the air, the spirit that is now at work in the sons of disobedience—among whom we all once lived in the passions of our flesh, carrying out the desires of the body and the mind, and were by nature children of wrath, like the rest of mankind" (Eph. 2:1-3).

The question, then, is: What can Satan do to Christians? He can communicate thoughts with us. He can plant messages in our brains. I believe the Bible calls these flaming darts: "In all circumstances take up the shield of faith, with which you can extinguish all the flaming darts of the evil one" (Eph. 6:16). We are to reject these lies and push them out with the truth of God's Word. The problem is that these untruths are mixed with truth. The best way to readily detect a counterfeit $20 bill is to study the real one in depth. Only knowing and using the truth of the Word of God can help us detect and remove lies.

Here are some possible outcomes if Christians do not remove the wrong thinking or lies from their minds. Believers can give an opportunity to the devil: "Be angry and do not sin; do not let the sun go down on your anger, and give no opportunity to the devil" (Eph. 4:26-27). Believers can be ensnared by the devil: "Moreover, he must be well thought of by outsiders, so that he may not fall into disgrace, into a snare of the devil" (1 Tim. 3:7). When believers find themselves in the snare of the devil, they will be manipulated by the enemy to do his will: "And the Lord's servant must not be quarrelsome but kind to everyone, able to teach, patiently enduring evil, correcting his opponents with gentleness. God may perhaps grant them repentance leading to a knowledge of the truth, and they may come to their senses and escape from the snare of the devil, after being captured by him to do his will" (2 Tim. 2:24-26). It is fair to say that in this context, Satan's will is to oppose the servants of God and the work of God. If you have been in ministry for a while, you likely have at least one story about a Christian who opposed you and your ministry.

Believers involved in ministry will receive in their minds flaming darts of the enemy. When a believer does not resist the devil and welcomes the flaming darts, embraces the lies, and dwells on the lies instead of rejecting them, that person's thinking becomes incorrect, his emotions become quite negative, he makes wrong decisions, and his relationships and ministry suffer. That believer can still serve with some effectiveness benefiting from his gifts, but it is just a matter of time before things begin to fall apart because God is not pleased, and He is removing His blessing.

There are many examples in the Bible of people who were targeted with flaming darts and, instead of rejecting them, they embraced them. Of course, the greatest example is found in the very beginning of our Bibles in Genesis 3. Satan's words to Eve mixed lies with truth. Eve (and Adam) neglected to reject the lies and instead embraced them. They made the decision to do what Satan told them to do. They sinned and opposed the will of God. This is a clear example of being captured in the snare of the devil, resulting in doing the will of Satan. When God showed up and asked them what they had done, Eve responded, "The serpent deceived me, and I ate" (Gen. 3:13). As Christians, we must discern that deception very early—before the sin occurs.

The big outstanding question is: "How do we resist the devil?" The Apostle Paul said that we don't do battle with the enemy with our flesh.

> *For though we walk in the flesh, we are not waging war according to the flesh. For the weapons of our warfare are not of the flesh but have divine power to destroy strongholds. We destroy arguments and every lofty opinion raised against the knowledge of God, and take every thought captive to obey Christ.*
>
> *2 Corinthians 10:3-5*

There are some things we can do by faith to remove the lies of the enemy and "take every thought captive to obey Christ" (v. 5).

First, by faith we need to put on the armor of God. This instruction is found in Ephesians 6:10-18. This teaching both begins and ends with prayer. It is an act of faith. This is not a text for us to simply know: The armor of God is meant to be put on by faith. "Put on the whole armor of God, that you may be able to stand against the schemes of the devil" (Eph. 6:10). I want to share with you Warren

Wiersbe's "Prayer for the Armor of God." It is simple, biblical, and powerful. It would be good to place it in a visible location to remind yourself each day to put on the armor of God.

> *Father, thank you for the provision you have made for victory over Satan. Now, by faith, I put on the girdle of truth. May my life today be motivated by truth. Help me to maintain integrity. By faith, I put on the breastplate of righteousness. May my heart love that which is righteous and refuse what is sinful. Thank you for the imputed righteousness of Christ. By faith, I put on the shoes of peace. Help me to stand in Christ's victory today. Help me to be a peacemaker and not a troublemaker. By faith, I take the shield of faith. May I trust you and your Word today and not add fuel to any of Satan's darts. Thank you that I can go into this day without fear. By faith, I put on the helmet of salvation. May I remember today that Jesus is coming again. Help me to live in the future tense. Protect my mind from discouragement and despair. By faith, I take the sword of the Spirit. Help me to remember your Word and to use it today. Father, by faith I have put on the armor. May this be a day of victory. Through Jesus Christ, my Savior and my Lord. Amen.*[52]

Second, we must exercise faith in the Word of God to remove the lies of the enemy. Remember the text in 1 Peter 5:8-9: "Be self-controlled and alert. Your enemy the devil prowls around like a roaring lion looking for someone to devour. Resist him, standing firm in the faith." Part of resisting the devil is standing firm in the faith. Notice, also, the words of the Apostle Paul: "In all circumstances take up the shield of faith, with which you can extinguish all the flaming darts of the evil one" (Eph. 6:16). We stand with faith in God and His Word. With faith we must focus on the promises of God to remove the lies the enemy has planted in our minds.

There are hundreds of promises in the Bible. Our faith will be strengthened as we focus on the promises of God instead of the battles at hand. This is an important aspect of resisting the devil. In Matthew 4 Jesus was in the wilderness and was tempted by the devil. The temptation was real, but He was able not to sin. He taught us how to confront temptations. These are Jesus' answers to the temptations in the wilderness. Notice how He uses God's Word.

- "But he answered, 'It is written, "Man shall not live by bread alone, but by every word that comes from the mouth of God" (Matt. 4:4).
- "Jesus said to him, 'Again it is written, "You shall not put the Lord your God to the test" (Matt. 4:7).
- "Then Jesus said to him, 'Be gone, Satan! For it is written, "You shall worship the Lord your God and him only shall you serve""" (Matt. 4:10).

I would also add the importance of speaking the Word of God out loud. In the quietude of our thoughts, so many times the enemy distracts our reflection upon the Word with reflection on the problems at hand. God told Joshua, "This Book of the Law shall not depart from your mouth…" (Josh. 1:8). We need to speak aloud the truths of God's Word. Our ears need to hear it. Our minds need to hear it. Our hearts need to hear and believe it. Only the Word of God can remove the subtle lies of the enemy.

Third, we must rebuke the enemy in Jesus' name. Is this a biblical practice? Where in the Scriptures do we learn about this idea? In Matthew 4 Jesus was in the wilderness. Three times the Lord was tempted by the devil. The last temptation reads, "Again, the devil took him to a very high mountain and showed him all the kingdoms of the world and their glory. And he said to him, 'All these I will give you, if you will fall down and worship me'" (Matt. 4:8-9). During the two previous temptations, Jesus responded with the Word of God. How would he reply to this one? "Then Jesus said to him, "Be gone, Satan! For it is written, 'You shall worship the Lord your God and him only shall you serve'" (Matt. 4:10). The Lord again responded to the temptation with the truth of God's Word. But He added, "Be gone, Satan!" Do you know what happened after he said that? We read in verse 11, "Then the devil left him…." Not only did the devil leave at Christ's command, but: "behold, angels came and were ministering to him" (Matt. 4:11). We see in this text that Jesus has the authority to rebuke Satan.

There is another occasion where we see Jesus teaching us this concept by his own example. In Matthew 16:21, "Jesus began to show his disciples that he must go to Jerusalem and suffer many things from the elders and chief priests and scribes, and be killed, and on the third day be raised." Peter did not like what he heard. He did not want Jesus to die, and so he took matters into his own hands. "Peter took him aside and began to rebuke him, saying, 'Far be it from you, Lord! This shall never happen to you'" (Matt. 16:22). Peter received an idea from the devil: to keep Jesus from the cross, where He would die for our sins. Then Peter opened his mouth, and out came the devil's idea. Jesus immediately rebuked Satan: "But he turned and said to Peter, 'Get behind me, Satan! You are a hindrance to me…'" (Matt. 16:23). Once again, Jesus told Satan to move. Satan was in front of Jesus in the middle of the conversation and needed to move on, to move behind and away from Jesus.

Twice the Lord has given us an example of how to resist the devil. We do not have the authority to do it ourselves. But, as followers of Christ, we can speak the words Jesus spoke to the enemy. We do not personally have authority over the devil. Only the Lord has power over the devil. This means we should speak the words that Jesus spoke to the devil and add "in Jesus' name." Using the precious and powerful name of Jesus means we are claiming Jesus' authority over the enemy. For example, we can say, "Get behind me, Satan, in Jesus' name," or "In Jesus' name, get behind me, Satan," or "Be gone, Satan, in Jesus' name." I believe this type of command should be reserved for those very dark times in our life where we feel a darkness and oppression that differs from day-to-day spiritual warfare. It is in these very dark moments that so many people, including Christians, make some of the worst decisions, including suicide. We need to remember that the power of Christ is greater than the power of the enemy. Jesus is always victorious.

There have been three or four such dark moments in my life, and I can testify that God's Word is true and that the power of Christ is real. I know this is a difficult and heavy topic. I want to leave you with some Scripture to encourage you and give you hope:

> *"...The reason the Son of God appeared was to destroy the devil's work" (1 John 3:8). What a powerful thought! Christ came to destroy the works of the devil.*

> *"...On this rock I will build my church, and the gates of hell shall not prevail against it" (Matt. 16:18). The church will overcome the gates of hell.*

> *"You are from God, little children, and have overcome them; because greater is He who is in you than he who is in the world" (1 John 4:4). Christ in us is greater and more powerful than the enemy around us.*
>
> *"But thanks be to God, who gives us the victory through our Lord Jesus Christ" (1 Cor. 15:57). Jesus is always victorious.*
>
> *"But the Lord is faithful, and he will strengthen you and protect you from the evil one" (2 Thess. 3:3). The Lord is our refuge and protector from the evil one.*

I would like to finish this chapter with a reminder based on James 4:7: "Submit yourselves to God. Resist the devil, and he will flee from you." In order to resist the devil in this way, Christians must submit themselves to God and desire the rule and will of God for their lives. Give praise and glory to our Savior, who is victorious over Satan! "The Lord will rescue me from every evil deed and bring me safely into his heavenly kingdom. To him be the glory forever and ever. Amen" (2 Tim. 4:18).

Practical Helps for Leaders

Mental battles take place in every Christian's mind. This book has covered many ways to wage those battles and has offered some help to gain victory. There are some additional practical ideas I would like to cover in this section.

Counseling

When Christians are struggling for long periods of time with a disappointment, with discouragement, with anxiety, or with other personal issues and have tried unsuccessfully to improve, it is beneficial to consider biblical counseling with a licensed professional counselor. A trained and licensed Christian professional might be able to help you through this season of pain. I know a Christian woman who lost her parents when she was a young mother, and the sadness from becoming an orphan so early in life triggered a depression that lasted several years. What helped improve her quality of life was the help of a biblical counselor. Perhaps part of what you do in ministry is to counsel people, and so you have a hard time with the idea of seeking counsel yourself. It is still the right and healthy thing to do. Perhaps you can find a counselor located outside your city so your sessions feel a bit more private.

Health

So many times, our mental battles relate to fear, worry, anxiety, depression, etc. There could be a chemical imbalance in your body or perhaps a medical condition that needs to be addressed. It is important that you are under the medical supervision of a doctor. Undergoing a yearly physical, including blood work, can be a good starting point for your health maintenance. Sometimes medications are needed to help with a crisis or to help address a chemical imbalance. Don't hesitate to talk with your doctor about your mental health.

Boundaries

Ministry never ends. People in ministry are pulled for ministry needs at all hours of the day and night. You need to set and enforce boundaries. You need to protect your family time and your mind. I make a point of not reading work emails after a certain hour in the evening and on weekends. If I go on vacation, I tell my team I will not be reading emails, and I tell my assistant that I can be contacted by text if there is an emergency. Then I define "emergency" as "the building is on fire."

Set healthy boundaries. Delegate responsibilities when you are absent so that ministry doesn't stop and so that you are able to rest. You will find that you will be much healthier, which will allow you to serve effectively in ministry. Also, your family, your body, and your mind will thank you.

Workaholism

Some people in ministry work all day, every day. Some of the workaholics I know are that way for several reasons. One lives in a country where working hard is part of the culture, another one has attached his own significance to his performance, and another has the energy of three people. All of them love the Lord and want to make a difference for the Gospel. There is only one issue: the need for rest. God rested on the seventh day not because He was tired, but because He wanted to model rest for us. If you press too hard, eventually something will give out, whether it is your health, your mind, your family, or your relationship with God.

Rest

From God's perspective, rest is important. Ministry leaders need both physical rest and mental rest. Jesus led his disciples to do the same thing. "And he said to them, 'Come away by yourselves to a desolate place and rest a while.' For many were coming and going, and they had no leisure even to eat" (Mark 6:31). The needs of ministry never end. People in ministry need to plan for seasons of rest. Set aside at least one day a week for rest. Weekends sometimes are not the best time to rest if you are in ministry—it depends on the type of ministry you have. Plan your vacations well in advance. Use all or most of your vacation days. Keep in mind that rest is not only physical. You need to rest your mind as well. Sitting in a chair on vacation with your mind racing about situations back at work is *not* rest. It is of great importance that we learn to rest in our minds by giving our concerns to the Lord and then leaving them there.

Sabbaticals

Some types of ministry positions are very tiring. Ministry leaders will give and give until they have nothing else to give. Leaders serving in front-line Gospel ministry wear down because of ministry mental battles. Mental and emotional exhaustion over time can cause people to give up and quit. Ministry leadership turnover is very taxing for leaders, at times involving moving the family to another area, and leaves the ministry without leadership for a period of time. The search for a replacement can be expensive, and the results are not always guaranteed. In most situations, it is better to retain your leaders, but something must be done to provide extended rest. I would encourage a well-planned sabbatical. As a matter of fact, I recommend a regular sabbatical every so many years. These can have a bit of structure so that there are some goals attached and some reporting. You will also need to take your responsibilities and divide them into three categories: one group waits until you return, another group will be completed by your peers, and a third group will be accomplished by those above you (for example, board members). The most important part of the sabbatical is for the leader to step away from the day-to-day activities of the ministry for a long period of time, approximately 60 to 90 days, to recharge the physical, emotional, and spiritual batteries.

Fellowship

Believe it or not, leadership positions in ministry can be lonely. So many times, leaders do not feel comfortable opening up about their struggles to those they lead. Besides the fellowship that the local church can provide, it is important for ministry leaders to fellowship with other ministry leaders. Perhaps regular in-person meetings or video conferencing meetings would accomplish this. Those regular contacts with other ministry leaders are a time to share burdens and to gain counsel and prayer support. This requires some vulnerability, but the dividends are wonderful. Lasting and meaningful relationships can come out of these interactions. Leaders need those.

Mentoring

The New Testament instructs the older generation to teach the younger generation. If you are a more experienced ministry leader, offer to a young ministry leader your availability to mentor him or her. If you are a younger leader, approach an experienced leader and ask for a mentoring relationship. These can be as formal or as informal as you want them to be. It is especially important for the young ministry leader to have a safe place to gain counsel in all areas of life: ministry, family, and personal. Much-needed leadership accountability can develop from these relationships. I strongly recommend these relationships to be between those of the same gender.

Member care

If you are leader with a staff team under you, be sure to provide care for your team members. Part of leadership in ministry is to make sure that staff members are cared for and not left alone carrying the heavy burdens that life can throw at them. This is part of obeying Paul's admonition in Galatians 6:2: "Bear one another's burdens, and so fulfill the law of Christ." It is not only what they can do for the ministry that is important. I have said to team members many times that they are more important than the work they do. What signals are you communicating to your team members? They have personal struggles, and they need encouragement and prayer support. Always take care and use wise boundaries when ministering to team members of the opposite gender. Respect your staff and yourself throughout this process just as you would do in the daily ministry you carry out. Never forget that no matter what you do in ministry, you are working "as for the Lord and not for men" (Col. 3:23). Otherwise, you can start a whole new mental battle that so many times ends in disaster.

Conferences

Ministry leaders need to be refreshed through regular conferences. Once or twice a year, ministry leaders need to participate in a conference with other ministry leaders. This should be a time of encouragement, refreshment, networking, sharpening skills, and gathering new ministry ideas. If there is not enough money in the budget to attend such a conference, find ways to be creative with your budget so your leaders can attend. Staff are the most important asset in any ministry. We must invest in them. Just like a bank account, you can only take out if you first put in. For our ministry leaders to minister and give left and right, we need to make deposits into their souls. The ministry I work for holds a Spiritual Renewal Conference in early December each year. Three Bible speakers are invited and music ministers as well. It is a wonderful time to fill our souls with God's Word, and it sets the tone for the new year of ministry.

Practical Helps for Followers

Mental battles are a challenge for all believers, but they seem to be more intense for ministry leaders. The world, the devil, and the flesh seem to attack those in ministry leadership in a stronger way. Perhaps the enemy knows that causing a leader to fail will most likely negatively impact many people. As a follower, you are not in a supervisor role to address all these areas, but you can be informed and show care by gently asking your leaders how they are doing.

We are motivated to bless our leaders by the words of the Apostle Paul: "We ask you, brothers, to respect those who labor among you and are over you in the Lord and admonish you, and to esteem them very highly in love because of their work. Be at peace among yourselves" (1 Thess. 5:12-13).

Be involved in ministry

Nothing encourages ministry leaders more than when their followers are involved in ministry, using the spiritual gifts God gave them, serving one another and growing in the faith while serving. So many times, ministry leaders do too much because few people are willing to help. Approach your ministry leaders and ask them how you can help make their load lighter.

Stay open to new ideas

From time to time, your ministry leaders will introduce new ministries or new ways to do ministry. Keep an open mind to those ideas. Human beings in general are creatures of habit and are uncomfortable with change. Stretch yourself and give the new way an opportunity to succeed. More than that, get involved and help the new idea flourish.

Don't gossip about leaders

Bring a concern kindly to your leaders. Do not talk about your concern to others behind leaders' backs. Nothing destroys unity faster than gossip. Go up the chain of command to address problems. If you go laterally to other individuals, you only make the problem bigger. Those who can fix the problem are up the chain of command. Start with your leaders. Approach them with a humble attitude.

Encourage your leaders

Kind words are a powerful and easy way to encourage. A nicely written note can provide encouragement in the present and into the future. Gift cards are very encouraging for leaders and their families. Be creative: There are many ways to encourage your leaders that are meaningful to them and their families. Be intentional about encouraging your leaders. Ministry leaders find themselves in many battles, and they need that encouragement.

Realistic expectations of your leaders

Every ministry leader has strengths and weaknesses; they are not perfect. Be realistic with your expectations. Don't compare your ministry leaders to previous leaders. Lower your expectations of your leaders, and don't put them on a pedestal. Raise your expectations of yourself: Get involved and help the ministry to succeed.

Marriage

Ministry puts a lot of pressure on marriages. Help your ministry leaders to take time away with their families and also to participate in marriage events, seminars, or conferences. Sometimes a gift card for ministry couples to go out to a restaurant can be a good practical help. Offering to watch their children so they can get away together will do wonders for their marriage.

Encourage vacations

If ministry leaders are not intentional about rest, they will eventually burn out. Make sure their vacation days are used up. Perhaps you know a family who can offer them a place to stay or some extra finances for their vacation. I remember, when my wife and I had been through an extremely difficult year, how blessed we were when a friend offered for us to stay at their condo for a week. That was a huge encouragement.

Pray for your leaders

Ministry leaders are typically in the middle of battles on a regular basis. They need your daily prayer support. Their families also need the prayer protection that can be provided through the prayers of God's people. Put up a couple of sticky notes to make sure you are reminded to pray for your leaders.

Regular rest

Make sure your ministry leaders are taking weekly time to rest and are not working seven days a week, burning the candle at both ends. Lack of rest over a long period of time will reduce leaders' effectiveness and will lead to burnout. Physical rest is important, but so is mental rest. When leaders are away, do not text them with problems; send those to other leaders who are standing in that gap.

Counseling

Many ministry leaders give counseling to people on a regular basis. There are times in life when their personal battles are intense, and ministry leaders require a visit to a counselor or therapist. Please do all you can to facilitate that and to show respect for a leader's choice to get help. Even doctors go to the doctor.

Boundaries

Ministry never ends. People in ministry are pulled for ministry needs at all hours of the day and night. Please guard ministry leaders' boundaries, such as needs for rest, family, etc. Leaders need to have time with their families so that their families and marriages remain healthy. Ask leaders for the most convenient times to contact them instead of making a habit of contacting them in the evenings.

Sabbaticals

Some types of ministry positions are very tiring. Ministry leaders will give and give until they have nothing else to give. It is important for leaders' long-term spiritual, mental, and emotional health to allow them to have a sabbatical every so many years. This is different from a vacation. Do not oppose it just because you may not get one at your secular work.

Coaching and accountability

Ministry leaders need time for relationships both with older leaders for the purpose of coaching and with a few select close ministry friends who will provide personal accountability. Ministry leadership can be a lonely activity. These key relationships provide vital fellowship to leaders.

Conferences

It is important for ministry leaders to be refreshed by participating in regular conferences. This can be a nice time away, but also will be a time rich in fellowship with other leaders. The content of the ministry conference will sharpen leaders' ministry skills and make that time away very valuable. Encourage your ministry leaders to participate in conferences.

Conclusion

Perfect peace is what we all desire. Isaiah tells us that perfect peace is found when our mind is stayed on God: "You keep him in perfect peace whose mind is stayed on you, because he trusts in you" (Isa. 26:3). Perfect peace sounds so wonderful. If we are honest, those moments of perfect peace seem to be temporary. We desire peace all the time, but while we are on this earth, it seems we go from those moments of peace to moments of turmoil and from moments of peace to moments of fear. It seems our hearts are on an emotional yo-yo. Most of the time our emotions are being impacted by our mental battles.

Peter showed us why it is easy to slide from peace into a mental battle. In the words of the Lord, a mental battle takes place when "you are not setting your mind on the things of God, but on the things of man" (Matt. 16:23). Through this book I have tried to help people involved in ministry to experience victory in their mental battles. We covered many different aspects of what it means to set our minds on the things of God. We looked at mental battles within yourself, battles with people, and battles with the enemy. It is my hope that in each chapter you found biblical principles that encouraged you on your journey to obtain help and victory in your mental battles.

I have heard it said that we should go through ministry with the end in sight. When we are on our deathbeds and our key priorities become as clear as they will ever be, what life and ministry priorities will rise to the top of the list? We ought to consider those now.

On December 18, 2021, a good friend of mine, Julie Spiegel, passed on to glory after a battle with stage IV cancer. She served the Lord for many years, and just before her retirement, she spent a few of those years as part of my leadership team. She was a single woman with a passion to serve God, especially to develop leaders. In her last days of life, we talked and texted back and forth. One day she told me something that I will never forget. I told her about the book I was writing, and 13 days before she died, she texted me this:

> *Moisés, sounds like a book I needed especially during the first part of my ministry when priorities were mixed up and burnout was an issue. If I was going to write a book... which I am not...I would add this... This week I was cleaning out a file drawer and found a stack of plaques and awards I received during my career as a teacher and in CEF. Most still in bubble wrap. I reread them all thinking over the honor received and the memories then wondered what am I going to do with them. With just a short time to live, I was decluttering. I knew no family members would want them. So later that day my brother came over and took them out to the garbage bin. Memories, career highlights, honors were all tossed. It was such a vivid reminder that only what is done for Christ will last. I will remember it for a long time.*[53]

Her statement impacted my heart in a powerful way. All the awards and honors were thrown in the trash as my friend, Julie, was getting ready to leave this earth to her celestial home. It reminded me that while we are alive and serving, we need to put the most important things first—all the rest will end up in the garbage bin anyway. So many of the things we battle with in our minds will end up in the garbage bin. We need to "pick our battles" carefully. Let's go through life releasing the minor things and focusing on the major things, those things that are truly important to God. Let's set our minds on the things of God and not on the things of men.

You cannot always change the circumstances that are causing mental battles for you and adding stress to your life. As you apply the principles covered in this book, it is my prayer that you will be able to resolve your mental battles with the help of the Lord and experience God's incredible peace. "And the peace of God, which surpasses all understanding, will guard your hearts and your minds in Christ Jesus" (Phil. 4:7).

Endnotes

[1] "Pastors Share Top Reasons They've Considered Quitting Ministry in the Past Year," Barna Group, April 27, 2022, https://www.barna.com/research/pastors-quitting-ministry/.
[2] James C. Dobson, *Straight Talk to Men: Recovering the Biblical Meaning of Manhood* (Nashville, TN: Word Publishing, 2000), 207-8.
[3] "Humility," Sermon Illustrations, July 18, 2022, http://www.sermonillustrations.com/a-z/h/humility.htm.
[4] Victor "Skip" Hessel, personal message to author, 2022.
[5] Warren W. Wiersbe and Lloyd M. Perry, *The Wycliffe Handbook of Preaching and Preachers* (Chicago: Moody Press, 1984), 243-55.
[6] Tim Hansel, "Humility," Sermon Illustrations, excerpt from *Eating Problems for Breakfast* (Word Publishing, 1988), 33-4, July 18, 2022, http://www.sermonillustrations.com/a-z/h/humility.htm.
[7] Warren W. Wiersbe and Lloyd M. Perry, *The Wycliffe Handbook of Preaching and Preachers* (Chicago: Moody Press, 1984), 243-55.
[8] Henry G Bosch, Our Daily Bread® Copyright © 1973 by Our Daily Bread Ministries, Grand Rapids, MI. Reprinted by permission. All rights reserved.
[9] Victor "Skip" Hessel, personal message to author, 2022.
[10] History.com editors, "Televangelist Jim Bakker Is Indicted on Federal Charges," History.com, November 13, 2009, https://www.history.com/this-day-in-history/jim-bakker-is-indicted-on-federal-charges.
[11] Max Lucado, *In the Eye of the Storm: A Day in the Life of Jesus* (Nashville, TN: Word Publishing, 1991), 153.
[12] William J. Bausch, *A World of Stories for Preachers and Teachers: And All Who Love Stories That Move and Challenge* (Blackrock, Co Dublin: Columba Press, 1998), 5-6.
[13] Allan C. Emery, *A Turtle on a Fencepost* (Waco: World Wide, 1979), 54.
[14] Henry G Bosch, Our Daily Bread® Copyright © 1995 by Our Daily Bread Ministries, Grand Rapids, MI. Reprinted by permission. All rights reserved.
[15] William Gurnall and J.C. Ryle, *The Christian in Complete Armour: or, A Treatise on the Saints' War with the Devil, Etc.* (London: independently published, 2012).
[16] William M. Anderson, "Fear of God," in *The Faith That Satisfies: Sermons of William M. Anderson, Jr.* (New York: Loizeaux, 1949), 26-7.
[17] Wayne Grudem, *Systematic Theology: An Introduction to Bible Doctrine* (Grand Rapids, MI: Zondervan Publishing House, 1994), 659.
[18] "John Laird Mair Lawrence," Westminster Abbey, July 21, 2022, https://www.westminster-abbey.org/abbey-commemorations/commemorations/john-laird-mair-lawrence.

[19] Henry G Bosch, Our Daily Bread® Copyright © 2001 by Our Daily Bread Ministries, Grand Rapids, MI. Reprinted by permission. All rights reserved.
[20] Michael Pritchard, "Michael Pritchard on Fear," Desire to Inspire Studios Foundation, March 18, 2020, YouTube video, https://www.youtube.com/watch?v=vjJRdat6gZw.
[21] Florence Huntington Jensen, *Hearts Aflame (second edition)* (Waukesha, WI: Metropolitan Church Association, 1932).
[22] Cora Tucker, personal message to author, 2022.
[23] Florence Huntington Jensen, *Hearts Aflame (second edition)* (Waukesha, WI: Metropolitan Church Association, 1932).
[24] Tim Hansel, *You Gotta Keep Dancin': In the Midst of Life's Hurts, You Can Choose Joy!* (Colorado Springs, CO: David C. Cook, 1985), 87.
[25] Warren W. Wiersbe and Lloyd M. Perry, *The Wycliffe Handbook of Preaching and Preachers* (Chicago: Moody Press, 1984), 243–55.
[26] Henry G Bosch, Our Daily Bread® Copyright © 1980 by Our Daily Bread Ministries, Grand Rapids, MI. Reprinted by permission. All rights reserved.
[27] G. Campbell Morgan, "Waiting for God," OChristian.com, July 31, 2023, http://articles.ochristian.com/article14291.shtml.
[28] Wayne Stiles, *Waiting on God: What to Do When God Does Nothing* (Grand Rapids, MI: Baker Publishing Group, 2015), 16.
[29] Ben Patterson, *Waiting: Finding Hope When God Seems Silent* (Downers Grove, IL: InterVarsity Press, 1989), 119.
[30] Anonymous, personal message to author, 2022.
[31] D. Chisholm, *The Catechism in Examples* (London: Burnes Oates and Washbourne, 1908), 56-7.
[32] John Calvin to William Farel, from Strasbourg, 24 October 1538, in *Selected Books of John Calvin: Tracts and Letters, Vol. 4*, eds. H. Beveridge and J. Bonnet, trans. D. Constable (Grand Rapids, Mich.: Baker Book House, 1983), 101-2.
[33] Ernest Hemingway, "The Capital of the World," in *The Complete Short Stories of Ernest Hemingway* (New York: Scribner, 2007), 29.
[34] Erwin W. Lutzer, *Putting Your Past Behind You: Finding Hope for Life's Deepest Hurts* (Chicago: Moody Publishers, 1990), 115.
[35] C.S. Lewis, *Mere Christianity* (New York: Collier Books, 1986), 89.
[36] "Aristides De Sousa Mendes: His Life and Legacy: Sousa Mendes Foundation," Sousa Mendes Foundation, October 19, 2022.https://sousamendesfoundation.org/aristides-de-sousa-mendes-his-life-and-legacy/.
[37] Peter Rollins, *The Idolatry of God: Breaking Our Addiction to Certainty and Satisfaction* (New York: Howard Books, a division of Simon & Schuster, Inc., 2013), 57-58.
[38] Donald G. Barnhouse, *Let Me Illustrate: More than 400 Stories, Anecdotes, and Illustrations* (Westwood, NJ: Revell, 1967), 305.

[39] Warren W. Wiersbe, *50 People Every Christian Should Know: Learning from Spiritual Giants of the Faith* (Grand Rapids, MI: Baker Books, a division of Baker Publishing Group, 2009), 136.
[40] "Human Stubbornness," *Closer Walk*, December 1991, https://bible.org/illustration/human-stubbornness.
[41] James Clark, *Dealing with Conflict Biblically* (Kansas City, MO: Calvary University Press, 2022).
[42] Eugene A. Nida, "Disappointment," Sermon Illustrations, July 18, 2022, excerpt taken from *Customs and Cultures: Anthropology for Christian Missions*, 5-6, http://www.sermonillustrations.com/a-z/d/disappointment.htm.
[43] *Oxford Pocket Dictionary of Current English*, s.v. "disappointment," July 16, 2023, https://www.encyclopedia.com/humanities/dictionaries-thesauruses-pictures-and-press-releases/disappointment.
[44] Oswald J. Smith, *The Story of My Life and Ministry* (Toronto: Peoples Press, 1955), 165.
[45] Charles R. Swindoll, *Improving Your Serve: The Art of Unselfish Living* (Waco, TX: W Publishing Group, 2004), 45-8.
[46] June Hunt, *Biblical Counseling Keys* (Dallas: Hope for the Heart, 1997), 3.
[47] Ibid, 9.
[48] Tim Kimmel, *Little House on the Freeway, revised edition* (Colorado Springs, CO: Multnomah, 2013), 50-55.
[49] June Hunt, *Biblical Counseling Keys* (Dallas: Hope for the Heart, 1997), 19.
[50] Erwin W. Lutzer, *Putting Your Past Behind You: Finding Hope for Life's Deepest Hurts* (Chicago: Moody Publishers, 1990), 115.
[51] Henry G. Bosch, *Our Daily Bread*® Copyright © 1992 by Our Daily Bread Ministries, Grand Rapids, MI. Reprinted by permission. All rights reserved.
[52] Warren W. Wiersbe, *The Strategy of Satan* (Carol Stream, IL: Tyndale House Publishers, Inc., 2011), 136-37.
[53] Julie Spiegel, personal message to author, December 18, 2021.

Bibliography

Anderson, William M., Jr. "Fear of God." In *The Faith That Satisfies: Sermons of William M. Anderson, Jr.*, 26 27. New York: Loizeaux, 1949.

Bacall, A. "Over Expecter." Cartoon. *www.Cartoonstock.com*, n.d.

Barnhouse, Donald G. *Let Me Illustrate: More than 400 Stories, Anecdotes, and Illustrations*, 305. Westwood, NJ: Revell, 1967.

Bausch, William J. *A World of Stories for Preachers and Teachers: And All Who Love Stories That Move and Challenge*. Blackrock, Co Dublin: Columba Press, 1998.

Bosch, Henry G. *Our Daily Bread.* Grand Rapids, MI: Our Daily Bread Ministries, 1984.

Calvin, John, to William Farel, from Strasbourg, 24 October 1538. In *Selected Books of John Calvin: Tracts and Letters, Vol. 4*, edited by H. Beveridge and J. Bonnet, trans. D. Constable, 101-2. Grand Rapids, Mich.: Baker Book House, 1983.

Chisholm, D. In *The Catechism in Examples*, 56–7. London: Burnes Oates and Washbourne, 1908.

Clark, James. *Dealing with Conflict Biblically*. Kansas City, MO: Calvary University Press, 2022.

Dobson, James C. *Straight Talk to Men: Recovering the Biblical Meaning of Manhood*, 207–8. Nashville, TN: Word Publishing, 2000.

Emery, Allan C. *A Turtle on a Fencepost*. Minneapolis: World Wide, 1979.

Grudem, Wayne. *Systematic Theology: An Introduction to Bible Doctrine*, 659. Grand Rapids, MI: Zondervan Publishing House, 1994.

Gurnall, William, and J.C. Ryle. *The Christian in Complete Armour; or, A Treatise on the Saints' War with the Devil, Etc.* London, 2012.

Hansel, Tim. *Eating Problems for Breakfast: A Simple, Creative Approach to Solving Any Problem*, 33–4. Dallas: Word Publishing, 1988.

Hansel, Tim. *You Gotta Keep Dancin': In the Midst of Life's Hurts, You Can Choose Joy!* Colorado Springs, CO: David C. Cook, 1985.

Hemingway, Ernest. "The Capital of the World." In *The Complete Short Stories of Ernest Hemingway*, 29. New York: Scribner, 2007.

Hession, Roy. *Calvary Road*. Fort Washington, PA: CLC Publications, 2016.

History.com Editors. "Televangelist Jim Bakker Is Indicted on Federal Charges." Accessed November 13, 2009. https://www.history.com/this-day-in-history/jim-bakker-is-indicted-on-federal-charges.

"Human Stubbornness." *Closer Walk*, December 1991.

"Humility." Sermon Illustrations. Accessed August 2, 2023. http://www.sermonillustrations.com/a-z/h/humility.htm.

Hunt, June. *Biblical Counseling Keys*. Dallas: Hope for the Heart, 1997.

Jensen, Florence Huntington. *Hearts Aflame (second edition)*. Waukesha, WI: Metropolitan Church Association, 1932.

Kimmel, Tim, ed. *Little House on the Freeway, revised edition*, 56–61. Colorado Springs, CO: Multnomah Books, 2013. Kindle.

Lewis, C.S. *Mere Christianity*, 89. New York: Collier Books, 1986.

Lucado, Max. *In the Eye of the Storm: A Day in the Life of Jesus*, 153. Nashville, TN: Word Publishing, 1991.

Lutzer, Erwin W. *Putting Your Past Behind You: Finding Hope for Life's Deepest Hurts*, 115. Chicago: Moody Publishers, 1990.

Morgan, G. Campbell. "Waiting for God."OChristian.com. Accessed July 31, 2023. http://articles.ochristian.com/article14291.shtml.

Nida, Eugene A. "Disappointment." Sermon Illustrations, excerpt from *Customs and Cultures: Anthropology for Christian Missions*, 5-6. Accessed July 18, 2022. http://www.sermonillustrations.com/a-z/d/disappointment.htm.

"Pastors Share Top Reasons They've Considered Quitting Ministry in the Past Year." Barna Group. Accessed April 27, 2022. https://www.barna.com/research/pastors-quitting-ministry/.

Patterson, Ben. *Waiting: Finding Hope When God Seems Silent*, 119. Downers Grove, IL: InterVarsity Press, 1989.

Pritchard, Michael. "Michael Pritchard on Fear." Desire to Inspire Studios Foundation. March 18, 2020. YouTube video. https://www.youtube.com/watch?v=vjJRdat6gZw.

Rollins, Peter. *The Idolatry of God: Breaking Our Addiction to Certainty and Satisfaction*. New York: Howard Books, a division of Simon & Schuster, Inc., 2013.

Smith, Oswald J. *The Story of My Life and Ministry*. Toronto: Peoples Press, 1955.

Sousa Mendes Foundation. "Aristides de Sousa Mendes: His Life and Legacy: Sousa Mendes Foundation." Accessed October 19, 2022. https://sousamendesfoundation.org/aristides-de-sousa-mendes-his-life-and-legacy/.

Stiles, Wayne. *Waiting on God: What to Do When God Does Nothing*, 16. Grand Rapids, MI: Baker Publishing Group, 2015.

Swindoll, Charles R. *Improving Your Serve: The Art of Unselfish Living*, 45–8. Waco, TX: W Publishing Group, 2004.

Westminster Abbey. "John Laird Mair Lawrence." Accessed July 21, 2022. https://www.westminster-abbey.org/abbey-commemorations/commemorations/john-laird-mair-lawrence.

Wiersbe, Warren W. *50 People Every Christian Should Know: Learning from Spiritual Giants of the Faith*, 136. Grand Rapids, MI: Baker Books, a division of Baker Publishing Group, 2009.

Wiersbe, Warren W. *The Strategy of Satan*, 136–7. Carol Stream, IL: Tyndale House Publishers, Inc., 2011.

Wiersbe, Warren W., and Lloyd M. Perry. In *The Wycliffe Handbook of Preaching and Preachers*, 243–55. Chicago: Moody Press, 1984.

About the Author

Rev. Moisés Esteves was born and raised in Portugal. He graduated from the Portuguese Bible Institute and Calvary University. He served for thirty years in the USA on staff with Child Evangelism Fellowship in several capacities, including Vice President of USA Ministries, Vice President of International Ministries and Executive Vice President. Currently he serves as a missionary pastor in Portugal. Moisés and Maryjane have four grown children and two grandchildren.

If you want to contact Moisés, send him an email at moisespesteves@gmail.com.

www.ingramcontent.com/pod-product-compliance
Lightning Source LLC
LaVergne TN
LVHW010656110826
845149LV00014B/3113